OLD
TESTAMENT
WORDS
for Today

OLD
TESTAMENT
WORDS
for Today

100 Devotional Reflections

WARREN W. WIERSBE

BakerBooks

a division of Baker Publishing Group
Grand Rapids, Michigan

© 2013 by Warren W. Wiersbe

Published by Baker Books
a division of Baker Publishing Group
P.O. Box 6287, Grand Rapids, MI 49516-6287
www.bakerbooks.com

Printed in the United States of America

Library of Congress Cataloging-in-Publication Data
Wiersbe, Warren W.
    Old Testament words for today : 100 devotional reflections from the Bible / Warren W. Wiersbe.
        pages cm
    ISBN 978-0-8010-1536-6 (pbk.)
        1. Bible. Old Testament—Meditations. 2. Bible. Old Testament—Devotional use. I. Title.
    BS1151.55.W54 2013
    242'.5—dc23   2013002680

13   14   15   16   17   18   19   7   6   5   4   3   2   1

Preface

If you know how to select them, five words can express unforgettable, life-changing thoughts.

Thomas Jefferson put five words into the Declaration of Independence that declared liberty for the American colonies: "We hold these truths to be self-evident, that *all men are created equal*." Abraham Lincoln quoted those five words in his famous Gettysburg Address.

"*A specter is haunting Europe*" are the words Karl Marx and Friedrich Engels chose to open their *Communist Manifesto*, a small book whose message changed the map of Europe.

On June 18, 1940, Prime Minister Winston Churchill heartened the British people with a speech that concluded with five unforgettable words: "Let us therefore brace ourselves to our duty, and so bear ourselves that, if the British Commonwealth

5

and its Empire lasts for a thousand years, men will still say, '*This was their finest hour.*'"

The Bible contains many memorable five-word statements that are "living and powerful" (Heb. 4:12), inspired words that the Holy Spirit can use to direct us in today's chaotic world. In this book, I have provided meditations based on one hundred of these phrases as they are found in the Old Testament, using the New King James Version of the Scriptures.

I trust that as you meditate on God's Word and ponder my words, the Spirit of God will enlighten you and encourage you, enabling you to discover the will of God and enjoy doing it.

Warren W. Wiersbe

OLD
TESTAMENT
WORDS
for Today

1

Then the serpent said to the woman, *"You will not surely die."*

GENESIS 3:4

God put our first parents into a lovely garden where all their needs were met and they had the privilege of fellowshipping with him and serving him. The enemy was prepared to attack, as he always is, and from this event we can get the instructions we need to obey to defeat him.

Don't give Satan a foothold. One of Adam's responsibilities was to "keep" the garden (Gen. 2:15), which means to guard it. It's the same word used in Genesis 3:24, "to guard the way to the tree of life." It seems that Adam was not with his wife at that time, so she was an easier target for the evil one. Ephesians 4:27 warns us not to "give place to the devil," for all he needs is a small foothold and he can begin to wage war. Even today, his servants stealthily creep in and cause trouble (2 Tim. 3:6; Jude 4). Cultivating a lustful or unkind thought can provide a foothold, and so can deliberately refusing to do God's will.

Don't listen to Satan's offers. Satan is a counterfeiter and a masquerader who never reveals his true nature. He can even come as an angel of light (2 Cor. 11:14) and lead us astray. We can tell when Satan is at work because he questions God's Word and encourages us to deny the authority of Scripture, asking us, "Has God indeed said . . . ?" Satan first questions the Word, then denies the Word, then substitutes his own lies. Our reply must be, "Yes, God *did* say, and I am going to respect it!" We must immediately turn to the Lord in prayer and seek his wisdom. He will remind us of what we have learned from the Scriptures and we can use the sword of the

Spirit to defeat Satan, as Jesus did when Satan attacked him (Eph. 6:17; Matt. 4:1–11). It's important that we hide God's Word in our hearts, because this will enable us to overcome him (Ps. 119:11).

Remind yourself of God's rich blessings. A temptation is Satan's offer to give you something he claims that God hasn't given you. When Satan tempted Jesus, he suggested, "Your Father just said you were his beloved son. If he loves you, why are you hungry?" The warnings against temptation found in James 1:12–15 are followed by reminders that we are the recipients of God's good and perfect gifts (vv. 16–18). A temptation is Satan's cheap substitute for the real gifts from heaven the Father has given us. The devil wanted Jesus to transform stones into bread, but Jesus preferred the nourishing bread of life, the Word of God (Matt. 4:4).

First Timothy 2:14 reminds us that Eve was deceived by Satan, but when Adam showed up, he sinned with his eyes wide open because he wanted to remain with his wife. It was his deliberate disobedience that plunged the human race into sin and judgment (Rom. 5:12–21). It was our Lord's obedience and death on the cross that saved us from condemnation and made us the children of God.

Resist the devil and he will flee from you.

James 4:7

And take . . . the sword of the Spirit, which is the word of God.

Ephesians 6:17

2

> Then the LORD said to Cain, "Where is Abel your brother?" He said, "I do not know. *Am I my brother's keeper?*"

GENESIS 4:9

Like Cain and Abel, you and I came into this world as *children of Adam* and, like every baby born before us, we were born *receivers*. Our physical life and genetic structure were given to us by the Lord through our ancestors (Ps. 139:13–16). But spiritually speaking, we were born "by nature children of wrath," and as we grew older, we became "sons of disobedience" (Eph. 2:1–3). Like those two brothers, we are all sinners by nature and sinners by choice. Because of what we are and what we do, we need a Savior.

But we can be *believers*, be born again and become *children of God*, as did Abel. He admitted he was a sinner and by faith brought a blood sacrifice to offer to the Lord (Heb. 11:4). Just as we received human life at birth, so we receive eternal life in a new birth through faith in Jesus Christ, who gave himself as a sacrifice for our sins. Cain had no faith. He did not confess he was a sinner and therefore brought, not a blood sacrifice, but the works of his own hands from the earth. "For by grace you have been saved through faith, and that not of yourselves; it is the gift of God, not of works, lest anyone should boast" (Eph. 2:8–9).

Cain was not a believer, and he became a *deceiver, a child of the devil*! "For this is the message that you heard from the beginning, that we should love one another, not as Cain who was of the wicked one and murdered his brother" (1 John 3:11–12). A child of the devil is someone who rejects Jesus Christ but practices "religion" as a counterfeit Christian. Satan has a family (Gen. 3:15). Both John the Baptist and

10

Jesus called the Pharisees a "brood of vipers"—and Satan is the serpent (Matt. 3:7–9; 12:34; 23:33). Jesus also called them "sons of hell" (Matt. 23:15). It was the Pharisees who crucified Jesus, and the apostle Paul experienced "perils among false brethren" (2 Cor. 11:26; *see* Acts 20:29–31; 1 John 2:18–23). A godly and experienced evangelist told me, "If loving one another is the mark of a believer, then I don't think half of the people who belong to our local churches are truly born again."

But back to Cain and his question: "Am I my brother's keeper?" Is there a bit of sarcasm hidden in it? For his brother was a keeper of sheep (Gen. 4:2), and Cain may have meant, "Am I the keeper's keeper?" The answer of course is, "Yes!" The two great commandments are to love the Lord and to love your neighbor, and our neighbor is anybody who needs our help (Luke 10:25–37). As members of the human family, we should care for one another, and as members of God's family, we should love and serve one another (Gal. 5:13). Satan is a liar and a murderer (John 8:37–45) and his child Cain was like his father.

> Therefore as we have opportunity, let us do good to all, especially to those who are of the household of faith.
>
> Galatians 6:10

3

I will make you a great nation; I will bless you and make your name great; and *you shall be a blessing.*

Various forms of the word *bless* are used over four hundred times in the Bible, and we often use them in our ministries and conversations—and especially in our prayers. A *blessing* is something that God is, does, or says that glorifies him and edifies his people. The apostle Paul didn't think his thorn in the flesh was a blessing and asked God three times to remove it, but the thorn turned out to be a blessing both to Paul and to the church (2 Cor. 12:7–10). Peter tried to dissuade Jesus from going to the cross (Matt. 16:21–28), but what Jesus accomplished at Calvary has given blessing to the world for generations and will bless his people for eternity.

The blessings God gives us must in turn become blessings to others, because Christians are supposed to be channels, not reservoirs. To receive God's blessings and then selfishly keep them is to violate one of the basic principles of the Christian life. "The generous soul will be made rich, and he who waters will also be watered himself" (Prov. 11:25). We are blessed so that we might be a blessing.

Because Abraham and Sarah believed God and obeyed him, God blessed them and made them a blessing to the whole world. From them came the nation of Israel, and Israel gave the world the knowledge of the one true and living God. Through Israel came the Bible and Jesus Christ, the Savior of the world. Without the witness of Israel, the Gentile world today would be comprised of ignorant, idol-worshiping people "having no hope and without God in the world" (Eph. 2:12). Instead, "those who are of faith are blessed with believing Abraham" (Gal. 3:9).

Abraham blessed his nephew Lot and gave him first choice of the land in Canaan (Gen. 13). He also rescued Lot when he became a prisoner of war (Gen. 14), and because of Abraham's intercession, Lot was spared when Sodom was destroyed (Gen. 19:1–29). Unfortunately, Lot didn't follow his uncle's example of faith and ended up in a cave, drunk and committing incest (Gen. 19:30–38). Lot and his descendants brought trouble to Israel, not blessing.

But there were at least three occasions when even godly Abraham failed to be a blessing. Instead of trusting the Lord, Abraham tried to escape a famine by going to Egypt, and there he lied and caused a plague (Gen. 12:10–20). He also lied to the king of Gerar (Gen. 20:1–18). He tried to obtain the promised son his own way and brought division into his household (Gen. 16). We cannot be a blessing either at home or away from home if we are not walking with the Lord.

We all want to *receive* blessings from the Lord, but not everybody wants to *be* a blessing to others. That's one difference between a river and a swamp. The godly believer in Psalm 1 received blessing from God and then became like a tree, sharing the blessing with others. An English proverb says, "He who plants trees loves others besides himself." That proverb also applies to Christians, who should share like fruitful trees.

Freely you have received, freely give.

Matthew 10:8

13

4

> But as for you, you meant evil against me; but *God meant it for good*, in order to bring it about as it is this day, to save many people alive.

This statement is the Old Testament version of Romans 8:28, "And we know that all things work together for good to those who love God, to those who are the called according to His purpose." From our point of view, people, circumstances, and even the Lord may seem to be against us; but as children of God, we know that our heavenly Father is in control. We are sure that he loves us and knows what is best for us. Joseph is a great example of this truth.

At home, Joseph was pampered by his father, Jacob, and hated by his ten older brothers, who sold him into slavery when he was seventeen years old. In Egypt, his master's wife tried to seduce him and he was put into prison. But when he was thirty years old, Joseph was set free from both prison and slavery and Pharaoh appointed him second ruler of Egypt! Twice Joseph's brothers came to Egypt for food, and Joseph used their visits to work on their hearts and bring them to repentance. He revealed himself to them, forgave them, and told them to bring Jacob and all their families to Egypt where he would care for them. When Jacob died seventeen years later, the brothers feared that Joseph might punish them, but Joseph assured them that all that had happened was from the Lord. In the years that followed, God used Joseph to rescue the Hebrew people from extinction.

What God did was good for Joseph and helped to prepare him to be a leader. Had Joseph stayed home, his father's pampering would probably have ruined him. "It is good for a man to bear the yoke in his youth" (Lam. 3:27). Joseph's suffering made him a man of God and one of the greatest types of Jesus found in Scripture. God's plan was also good for Joseph's brothers and brought them out of their scheming ways and into repentance. From these men came the twelve tribes of Israel. When he was younger, Jacob had done his share of scheming and deceiving, and now he had paid for it. God gave him seventeen years of joy and peace with his entire family. God's plan was certainly good for Egypt too as Joseph managed the food supply. All these benefits have touched our world today, for "salvation is of the Jews" (John 4:22).

Have you ever said with Jacob, "All these things are against me" (Gen. 42:36)? Actually, all that happened to Joseph was working *for* him and his family—*and for us!* The next time we question the Lord because life is difficult and we can't understand his ways, let's remember young Joseph's trials and God's gracious, providential control of all things. We don't need to see or feel that God is working all things together for good because we *know* he is!

> It is good for me that I have been afflicted,
> That I may learn Your statutes.
>
> Psalm 119:71

> Behold, God is my salvation,
> I will trust and not be afraid.
>
> Isaiah 12:2

5

Now the blood shall be a sign for you on the houses where you are. And *when I see the blood*, I will pass over you; and the plague shall not be on you to destroy you when I strike the land of Egypt.

EXODUS 12:13

The unenlightened secular mind doesn't understand the importance of sacrificial blood in the Bible. Some liberal theologians call evangelical Christianity a "slaughterhouse religion," and many people reject the cross of Christ but still try to follow his ethical teachings. "For the message of the cross is foolishness to those who are perishing, but to us who are being saved it is the power of God" (1 Cor. 1:18). Rejecting the blood means rejecting Jesus and eternal salvation.

God saw the blood on the door. That blood bore witness to the Egyptians that judgment was coming, but it gave confidence and peace to the Jews behind the door. If the blood was on the door, they knew the angel of death would "pass over" their homes and the firstborn would not die. Blood on your neighbor's door would not suffice; you had to make it personal. Note the sequence in Exodus 12:3–5: "a lamb . . . the lamb . . . your lamb." The lamb pictured Jesus, the lamb of God who died for the sins of the world (John 1:29; 1 Pet. 1:18–19).

God saw the blood on the ark of the covenant (Lev. 16:14). The annual Day of Atonement was a high day on the Jewish calendar, the only day of the year on which the high priest was permitted to enter the holy of holies. He first sacrificed a bull as a sin offering for himself and his family and sprinkled its blood on the mercy seat in the holy of holies. Then he sacrificed a goat as a sin offering for the people and sprinkled its blood on the mercy seat. He then laid his hands on a living goat, confessed the sins of the people, and sent the goat into the wilderness at the hand of a "suitable man" (v. 21). In the ark were the tables of the law, but when the Lord looked down, he didn't see the broken law. He saw the blood! Hallelujah!

God saw the blood on human bodies (Exod. 29:20; Lev. 14:14, 26–28). When Aaron and his sons were dedicated as priests, Moses put some of the blood of the sacrificial ram on the right ear, thumb, and big toe of each man, a symbol of total dedication to the Lord. This same procedure was used with the cleansed lepers so they could return to the camp (Lev. 14:14). When a sinner today trusts Christ, the blood is applied by the Spirit and the sinner is saved! When a believer confesses his or her sins to the Lord, the blood is applied and the sins are forgiven (1 John 1:6–8).

God saw the blood on the cross. It was there that the Lord reconciled "all things to Himself . . . having made peace through the blood of His cross" (Col. 1:20). Jesus gave us the Lord's Supper to remind us of the new covenant that he established through his blood (Luke 22:20). Jesus took the wounds (not scars!) of the cross to heaven so that his people will remember the price he paid to save us. We have been redeemed "with the precious blood of Christ" (1 Pet. 1:19).

The promise in 1 John is dependable.

If we confess our sins, He is faithful and just to forgive us our sins and to cleanse us from all unrighteousness.

1 John 1:9

6

On that day the priest shall make atonement for you, to cleanse you, *that you may be clean* from all your sins before the LORD.

LEVITICUS 16:30

The book of Leviticus was given to the Jewish priests and their people so that they might "distinguish between holy and unholy, and between unclean and clean" (Lev. 10:10; *see* 11:47); for God's command is, "You should therefore be holy, for I am holy" (11:45). That order was given not only to the Israelites, but also to the church (1 Pet. 1:13–16). In Scripture, sin is compared to dirt, and God's people today are probably more in danger of being defiled by the world, the flesh, and the devil than were the ancient Jews (Eph. 2:1–3; 5:1–14). God taught his people spiritual discernment by giving them rules related to diet, personal health, and hygiene.

Cleansed by water. Defilement is a picture of sin, but washing is a picture of forgiveness (Ps. 51:2, 7). In the Bible, water for drinking is a symbol of the Spirit of God (John 7:37–39), but water for washing pictures the Word of God. "You are already clean because of the word which I have spoken to you," said Jesus (John 15:3), and Paul wrote about "the washing of water by the word" (Eph. 5:25–27). In the Old Testament sanctuaries, there was a large basin full of clean water called the laver. There the priests washed their hands and feet regularly during their daily ministry, for if they did not, they were in danger of being judged by God (Exod. 30:17–21). Note that the priests were defiled *while they served the Lord in the sanctuary.*

Cleansed by blood. In the previous meditation, we touched upon the power of sacrificial blood to deliver God's people from bondage and judgment, as the blood of the lamb did for each Jewish household in Egypt. "According to the law almost all things are purified with blood, and without shedding of blood there is no remission" (Heb. 9:22). It was Jesus on the cross who "loved us and washed us from our sins in His own blood" (Rev. 1:5). We are justified (declared righteous) by his blood (Rom. 5:9) and also sanctified (made righteous) by his blood (Heb. 13:12). When we confess our sins to the Lord, he forgives us and cleanses us through the blood of Jesus Christ (1 John 1:5–10).

Cleansed by fire. This applied primarily to the metal spoils of battle (Num. 31:21–24), "everything that can endure fire." But it also reminds us that God sometimes puts us in the fires of tribulation so that we might be purified. "Before I was afflicted I went astray, but now I keep Your word" (Ps. 119:67, 71, 75; *see* Heb. 12:11; 1 Pet. 1:6–7). When we go through the fire, God is with us and will use us to glorify him (Isa. 43:2; Dan. 3:16–26).

Are we distinguishing between the clean and the unclean and choosing only the very best for our lives (Ezek. 22:23–31; 44:23)? If not, we may find ourselves in the furnace of affliction experiencing the chastening of the Lord (Heb. 12:1–11). This doesn't mean being condemned by a stern judge, but being "spanked" by a loving Father whose goal is "that we may be partakers of His holiness" (Heb. 12:10), knowing the difference between clean and unclean.

Now no chastening seems to be joyful for the present, but painful; nevertheless, afterward it yields the peaceable fruit of righteousness to those who have been trained by it.

Hebrews 12:11

7

> *You must not fear them*, for the LORD your God
> Himself fights for you.
>
> DEUTERONOMY 3:22

W hen Moses spoke these words, he was reviewing
for the new generation Israel's journey from
Egypt to Canaan. Their ancestors had defeated
the two great kings, Sihon and Og (Deut. 2:26–3:11), and
Moses used these triumphs to encourage Joshua to trust the
Lord, go into the Promised Land, and conquer it. You and I
aren't warring against great nations, but we do have to face
"the rulers of the darkness of this age" (Eph. 6:12) as we claim
our inheritance in Christ. We must not fear the enemy so
much as our own failure to claim all that God has for us (Heb.
4:1–9). This means we must understand three kinds of fear.

There are *normal fears that must energize us*. Every child
must be warned about the dangers involved in crossing the
street, playing with electricity or knives, going into deep water,
or swallowing poison. Fearing injury and death is normal,
and when we are in dangerous situations, this fear energizes
us to make changes and seek help. Frightened soldiers spread
discouragement, and discouraged soldiers are not likely to
win a war (Deut. 20:3–4, 8).

There are also *abnormal fears that can paralyze us*. My
thesaurus lists four pages of phobias, with four columns
of phobias on each page! My dictionary defines a phobia
as "an exaggerated, usually inexplicable and illogical fear
of a particular object, class of objects, or situation." If you
are afraid of bathing, you have ablutophobia, but if you are
afraid of dirt, you have mysophobia. Some people have lacha-
nophobia, which is fear of vegetables, but even more suffer
from acrophobia, the dread of high places.

But there is *a fear that stabilizes us* that every believer *must* cultivate, and that's *the fear of the Lord*; for the fear of the Lord is the fear that cancels every other fear. "Blessed is the man who fears the LORD, who delights greatly in His commandments" (Ps. 112:1). Read that entire psalm and you will discover that the fear of the Lord cancels our fears about our family (v. 2), poverty (v. 3), darkness (v. 4), dumb decisions (v. 5), and a host of other fears.

To fear the Lord does not mean to cringe and crawl for fear our Father will destroy us, but to practice loving respect and joyful obedience toward our heavenly Father because we love him and want to please him. Because of who God is, what his character is, and what his authority is over us, we must respect him and obey him. A. W. Tozer wrote in *The Root of the Righteous*, "No one can know the true grace of God who has not first known the fear of God." Once we know the fear of God, we need not fear the enemy; for the Lord will be fighting for us!

"The fear of the LORD is the beginning of knowledge, but fools despise wisdom and instruction" (Prov. 1:7). Knowledge is a grasp of the facts of the world, but wisdom is knowing how to use those facts to do God's will and glorify his name. "The fear of the LORD is the beginning of wisdom" (Ps. 111:10). Our greatest enemy is our ignorance of spiritual wisdom as found in the Word of God.

He will bless those who fear the LORD.

Psalm 115:13

8

> So *Joshua took the whole land*, according to all
> that the LORD had said to Moses; and Joshua
> gave it as an inheritance to Israel according to
> their divisions by their tribes. Then the land rested
> from war.
>
> JOSHUA 11:23

The theme of the book of Joshua is Israel's conquest of Canaan under the leadership of Joshua. The Israelites already *owned* the land because of God's promise to Abraham (Gen. 13:14–18), but now they were to *possess* the land and enjoy it. It's unfortunate that some lyricists and poets think that crossing the Jordan and entering Canaan is a picture of dying and going to heaven, but it's not. Certainly there won't be any wars in heaven! Rather, it's a picture of believers *today* who separate themselves from the old life (cross the Jordan) and claim by faith their spiritual inheritance in Christ. This decision leads to both battles and blessings, but our Joshua, Jesus Christ, gives us victory followed by rest (Heb. 4).

Joshua was God's chosen leader (Num. 27:12–23; Deut. 31:1–8), a godly man with years of experience as head of the army (Exod. 17:8–16) and as Moses's faithful servant (Exod. 33:7–11). He was wholly dedicated to the Lord and knew that he was second in command (Josh. 5:13–15). The Lord commanded him to "be strong and of good courage" (Josh. 1:6, 7, 9) because he had promised to give him success. In each of the books of Moses you will find promises from God that he would drive out the enemy and give Israel their land, and Joshua claimed these promises (Gen. 13:14–18; Exod. 23:20–33; 33:1–2; 34:10–14; Lev. 18:24–25; 20:23–24; Num. 33:50–56; Deut. 4:35–38; 7:17–26; 9:1–6). He didn't

22

have a road map or a travel guide, but he did have God's Word (Josh. 1:7–8). What an example for us to follow!

But Joshua was a humble leader, ready to admit his mistakes and not blame somebody else. After the great victory at Jericho, he didn't take time to seek God's guidance, and Israel experienced a humiliating defeat at Ai (Josh. 7). Joshua fell on his face to seek the Lord and God told him to get up, stop praying, and get rid of the sinner whose disobedience had caused the defeat. Later, he again ran ahead of the Lord and made a covenant of peace with Israel's enemies, the Gibeonites (Josh. 9). It's important that God's servants take time to wait on the Lord and not grow overconfident because of past victories.

Joshua was a man of faith, and if anybody needs faith, it's leaders. "By faith the walls of Jericho fell down after they were encircled for seven days" (Heb. 11:30). Faith accepts God's strategy, no matter how bizarre it may appear, and obeys God's orders. Joshua even had the faith to call upon God to lengthen the day to give the army time to defeat the enemy (Josh. 10).

Joshua conquered the land, but, alas, not all the tribes claimed all their territory (Judg. 1:27–36). But has the church today claimed all that Jesus purchased for us on the cross? What we need are more people like Joshua who believe God and help others claim their inheritance.

> Finally, all of you be of one mind, having compassion for one another; love as brothers, be tenderhearted, be courteous; not returning evil for evil or reviling for reviling, but on the contrary blessing, knowing that you were called to this, that you may inherit a blessing.
>
> 1 Peter 3:8–9

9

> Then the LORD turned to him and said, "Go in this might of yours, and you shall save Israel from the hand of the Midianites. *Have I not sent you?*"
>
> JUDGES 6:14

I f we had been Gideon's neighbors, we would never have suspected that one day he would become a great general and a famous judge in Israel, but that's just what happened. When he was hiding in the winepress threshing wheat, it shocked Gideon that the Lord called him a "mighty man of valor" (Judg. 6:12). It must have amazed his friends that he had the courage to destroy the Baal idol and erect an altar to the Lord, and then he assembled a small army that defeated the Midianites. What was the secret of this dramatic transformation? *He was sent by God and trusted God to keep his promises.* The issue isn't who we are or what we can do but rather *have we been sent by God?*

However, at the beginning of this encounter with God, Gideon's unbelief almost ruined everything. "If the LORD is with us, why then has all this happened to us? And where are all His miracles. . . . But now the LORD has forsaken us" (v. 13). Gideon's mistake was to look at *his circumstances* instead of looking to God and obeying him. Our sovereign Lord is never hindered by circumstances, for he can do the impossible. When you live by faith in the true and living God, you don't ask questions. You trust promises.

Then Gideon looked at *himself* and became even more discouraged. "O my Lord, how can I save Israel? Indeed, my clan is the weakest in Manasseh, and I am the least in my father's house" (v. 15). But God had already called him a "mighty man of valor," and what God says is always true.

God has chosen the foolish things of the world to put to shame the wise, and God has chosen the weak things of the world to put to shame the things that are mighty; and the base things of the world and the things which are despised God has chosen, and the things which are not, to bring to nothing the things that are, that no flesh should glory in His presence.

1 Corinthians 1:27–29

Gideon qualified, and so do we!

In Hebrews 11:32, Gideon is listed with other heroes of faith who did great things that glorified the Lord who had sent them. When God sends us, he goes with us and stays with us. God's promise, "I am with you," sustained them and it can sustain us today. The Lord gave that promise to Abraham (Gen. 26:3), Jacob (Gen. 31:3), Moses (Exod. 3:12), Joshua (Josh. 1:5, 9), Jeremiah (Jer. 1:8, 19), the apostle Paul (Acts 18:9–10), and to every Christian believer today (Heb. 13:5–6). "Have I not sent you?" and "I am with you" can transform any Christian!

A friend sent me a bit of poetry that I find summarizes this meditation:

> Look at circumstances and you'll be distressed;
> Look at yourself and you'll be depressed;
> But look in faith to Jesus and you'll be blessed.

Let us run with endurance the race that is set before us, looking unto Jesus, the author and finisher of our faith.

Hebrews 12:1–2

10

> *The LORD repay your work*, and a full reward be given you by the LORD God of Israel, under whose wings you have come for refuge.
>
> RUTH 2:12

The Lord *did* repay Ruth's work, but she could never have worked at all had she not first put her faith in the Lord, for "faith without works is dead" (James 2:26). Her testimony in Ruth 1:16–17 is one of the greatest in Scripture and her life one of the purest and sweetest. Because she trusted him, the Lord repaid her by bringing about some wonderful changes in her life.

The outsider came in. "An Ammonite or Moabite shall not enter the assembly of the LORD" (Deut. 23:3), but Ruth abandoned her idols and accepted the Lord, and as a Jewish proselyte was part of the nation. But even more, spiritually speaking she moved into the holy of holies in the tabernacle, under the wings of the cherubim that guarded the Ark of the Covenant (Ps. 36:7–8; 61:4; 91:1–4). I had a similar experience when I trusted Christ. "Now in Christ Jesus you who once were far off have been brought near by the blood of Christ" (Eph. 2:13).

The mourner found peace. The opening chapter of the book of Ruth is drenched in tears of farewell as Elimelech and Naomi and their two sons left Bethlehem, and then as Naomi's husband and sons died leaving three widows behind. Widows and lepers were at the bottom of the social scale in those days. Naomi decided to return to Bethlehem and Ruth insisted on accompanying her. When they arrived, Naomi told her friends, "Do not call me Naomi; call me Mara," which in Hebrew means *bitter* (Ruth 1:20). But Ruth had God's peace in her heart and immediately began to minister to her mother-in-law. Ruth's sister-in-law back in Moab may have remarried and found rest (1:9), but the rest Ruth experienced in Bethlehem was far greater.

The laborer experienced satisfaction. Ruth learned that the Hebrew law permitted the poor to glean among the sheaves during the harvest, and she wanted to care for Naomi the best she could. Here we see the providence of God, for she "just happened" to pick the fields of Boaz, one of Naomi's relatives, and Boaz "just happened" to arrive while she was working. It was "love at first sight," and he told her to work only in his fields. He commanded his workers to protect her and provide for her by purposely dropping some sheaves for her to pick up. Boaz made sure she rested and had something to eat and drink, and yet she was a stranger! She had found favor (grace) in his eyes (2:2, 10, 13), which is the way salvation always begins.

The "nobody" was highly honored. Ruth not only became a believer and a member of the Jewish community, but she married Boaz and gave birth to King David's grandfather! Even more, her name is found in the genealogy of our Lord Jesus Christ (Matt. 1:5). Ruth began as a poor widow (chap. 1) who lived on leftovers (chap. 2). She received gifts from Boaz (chap. 3) and then ended up marrying Boaz and sharing all his wealth (chap. 4). This is the grace of God! These were God's "repayments" until one day she arrived in heaven and received her "full reward."

Repayments down here and a full reward in heaven—what a gracious Master we serve! Let's be sure we are servants who deserve rewards.

Look to yourselves, that we do not lose those things we worked for, but that we may receive a full reward.

2 John 8

11

Talk no more so very proudly; let no arrogance
come from your mouth, for the LORD is the God
of knowledge; and *by Him actions are weighed.*

1 SAMUEL 2:3

Hannah was a godly woman who was misunderstood
and criticized. Her husband's second wife, Penin-
nah, made fun of her and drove her to tears because
Hannah had no children, and Eli the high priest thought she
was drunk. She was in the ranks with other believers who
were misunderstood and criticized, such as Joseph, David,
Jeremiah, Paul, and even our Lord Jesus Christ. (He was even
accused of being in league with Satan!) But the Lord heard
Hannah's prayers and gave her a son whom she named Samuel
and dedicated to God to serve in the tabernacle. Samuel became one of the spiritual giants in the Old Testament. These
words from Hannah's joyful song of praise will encourage us
when people misunderstand us and criticize us.

God knows the truth. He knows what other people think
and say, and he also knows what *you* think and say (Ps.
139:1–6). He knows what is in every heart (Acts 1:24). "And
there is no creature hidden from His sight, but all things are
naked and open to the eyes of Him to whom we must give
account" (Heb. 4:13). We don't even know our own hearts
(Jer. 17:9)! Peter thought he was ready to die for the Lord,
only to discover that he was about to deny him three times.
When people lie about you, you can be sure your heavenly
Father knows the truth and one day will settle accounts.

God weighs people and their actions. Evangelist D. L.
Moody used to say that converts should be weighed as well
as counted, and our Lord does weigh people and what they
say and do. "Surely men of low degree are a vapor, men of

28

high degree are a lie; if they are weighed on the scales, they are altogether lighter than vapor" (Ps. 62:9). "'Vanity of vanities,' says the Preacher; 'vanity of vanities, all is vanity'" (Eccles. 1:2). Solomon used the Hebrew word *hevel* thirty-eight times in Ecclesiastes, and it's translated "vanity, emptiness, futility." Life in the will of God is solid and satisfying, but life outside his will is empty and meaningless.

Before we speak, we should weigh our words, because God does. "The heart of the righteous studies how to answer," wrote Solomon (Prov. 15:28). We should also judge the words spoken in church lest they are not true to God's Word (1 Cor. 14:29). Jesus warns, "But I say to you that for every idle word men may speak, they will give account of it in the day of judgment" (Matt. 12:36). God weighs our motives (Prov. 16:2) and our hearts (Prov. 21:2; 24:12). He sees and hears what nobody else can see and hear.

God rewards the "weighty." If we use weighty materials as we serve the Lord—gold, silver, and costly stones, not wood, hay, and straw—then God will weigh it and we shall receive a reward; if not in this life, then in the next (1 Cor. 3:12–17; Eph. 6:8; Col. 3:23–24). Potiphar's wife lied about Joseph and had him imprisoned, but God honored Joseph. King Saul lied about David and tried to kill him, but David was vindicated. Even the Lord Jesus was vindicated in his resurrection and glorious ascension to heaven.

King Belshazzar thought he was wealthy and powerful, and by the standards of the world, he was. But God told him, "You have been weighed in the balances, and found wanting" (Dan. 5:27). That very night, he was slain. Don't weigh life on the world's scales; weigh life on God's scales. If we put Christ first, we have him—and everything else we need!

> But seek first the kingdom of God and His righteousness, and all these things shall be added to you.
>
> Matthew 6:33

> So his armorbearer said to [Jonathan], "Do all
> that is in your heart. Go then; *here I am with you,*
> *according to your heart.* "
>
> 1 SAMUEL 14:7

F ive simple monosyllables—"here I am with you"—but they helped make the difference between success and failure. Jonathan had already won a battle, for which his father, King Saul, took the credit (1 Sam. 13:1–4), but he didn't care who got the credit so long as God received the glory and Israel was protected. As God's people, we have always been in conflict with the enemies of the Lord and we have always been outnumbered. There were three kinds of Israelites on the battlefield that day, just as there are three kinds of "Christian soldiers" in the church today.

There are those who do nothing. King Saul was sitting under a tree, surrounded by six hundred soldiers, wondering what to do next. Leaders are supposed to *use* their offices and not just fill them (1 Tim. 3:13). God had given Saul position and authority but he seemed to have no vision, power, or strategy. He was watching things happen instead of making things happen, and spectators don't make much progress in life. Along with Saul and his small army were a number of Israelites who had fled the battlefield and hidden themselves, and some had even surrendered to the enemy! When Jonathan and his armorbearer started defeating the Philistines and the Lord shook the enemy camp, these quitters came out into the open and joined in the battle. Do you know any Christians like that? Are you one of them?

There are those who fear nothing. Jonathan had already won a battle against the Philistines and was a man of faith who was certain that the God of Israel would give his people victory. Perhaps he was leaning on God's promises in Leviticus 26:7–8, "You will chase your enemies, and they shall fall by the sword before you. Five of you shall chase a hundred, and a hundred of you shall put ten thousand to flight." He assured his armorbearer that "nothing restrains the LORD from saving by many or by few" (1 Sam. 14:6). Jonathan expected God to give him a sign that his strategy was right, and God did just that (vv. 9–14). God also caused an earthquake in the enemy camp that made the Philistines panic, and they began to attack each other; and the enemy army began to melt away (v. 16).

There are those who hold back nothing. Jonathan's armorbearer is mentioned nine times in this narrative but his name is never revealed. Like many people in Scripture, he did his job well but must remain anonymous until he is rewarded in heaven. Think of the lad who gave his lunch to Jesus and he fed five thousand people (John 6:8–11), or the Jewish girl who sent Naaman to Elisha to be healed of his leprosy (2 Kings 5:1–4), or Paul's nephew whose fast action saved Paul's life (Acts 23:16–22).

The armorbearer encouraged Jonathan and promised to stand by him. All leaders, no matter how successful, need others at their side who can help expedite their plans. Aaron and Hur held up Moses's hands as he prayed for Joshua and the Jewish army in battle (Exod. 17:8–16), and Jesus asked Peter, James, and John to watch with him as he prayed in the garden (Matt. 26:36–46). Blessed are those leaders who have dependable associates whose hearts are one with theirs and who hold back nothing but devotedly say, "I am with you." Jesus says that to us and he will help us to say it to others.

I am with you always, even to the end of the age.

Matthew 28:20

31

13

> Then one of the servants answered and said, "Look, I have seen a son of Jesse the Bethlehemite, who is skillful in playing, a mighty man of valor, a man of war, prudent in speech, and a handsome person; and *the* LORD *is with him.*"
>
> 1 SAMUEL 16:18

David had not yet killed Goliath, so he was not the popular hero he later became. But this anonymous servant had watched him and admired him, and was recommending him to minister to Saul during the king's hours of demonic distress. There were other young men in Israel who were musicians, warriors, good speakers, and handsome, but what impressed Saul's servant most was that the Lord was with David. The Lord had been with Saul, but had departed from him (1 Sam. 10:7; 16:14). The Lord had been with Abraham (Gen. 21:22), Isaac (Gen. 26:28), Jacob (Gen. 28:15), Joseph (Gen. 39:2–3, 21, 23), and Joshua (Josh. 1:5), so David was in distinguished company. There is no higher compliment than that the Lord is with you—but what does it mean?

It means spiritual character. When Samuel went to Jesse's house to anoint David king, he was impressed with each of Jesse's sons. But the Lord cautioned him not to go by appearances, for "the LORD looks on the heart" (1 Sam. 16:7). Years later, Asaph wrote of David, "So he shepherded them according to the integrity of his heart" (Ps. 78:72). Saul was a double-minded man with a proud heart who wanted honor before the people (1 Sam. 15:30), but David was humble and wanted to honor the Lord. He was a man of character, a man after God's own heart (13:14). Robert Murray M'Cheyne wrote, "It is not great talents God blesses so much as great likeness to Jesus."

It means divine power. Though probably only a teenager, David killed the giant Goliath using just a shepherd's sling.

He led his soldiers from victory to victory so that the women were singing his praises: "Saul has slain his thousands, and David his ten thousands" (18:7). This helped to ignite Saul's burning envy of David and his desire to kill him, but the Lord protected David. Whom the Lord calls, he empowers and enables, and David depended on God's power. David knew how to build leaders (chap. 23). The Lord was with him and he would never fail. David wrote, "You have armed me with strength for the battle" (Ps. 18:39).

It means opposition. The people of Israel loved and respected David, but Saul and his followers sought to kill him. Any true believer who honors the Lord and lets the light shine will be attacked by people who prefer the darkness (John 3:19–21). For perhaps seven years, Saul pursued David and his men, who moved from place to place and even lived in caves. You and I may not be pursued by armies, but "all who desire to live godly in Christ Jesus will suffer persecution" (2 Tim. 3:12).

It means lasting blessings. First Kings 2 records the death of David, but his name is found many times in the Bible after that. David blessed people after his death and is still blessing God's people today. He left both the blueprints for the temple and great wealth to build the temple (1 Chron. 28:11–20). He also left weapons for the army (2 Kings 11:10; 2 Chron. 23:9), musical instruments for the temple choirs (2 Chron. 29:26–27; Neh. 12:36), and psalms for them to sing. Many songs we sing today have their origin in the psalms of David. Our Savior Jesus Christ came through the line of David.

The gifts David bequeathed us are still blessing us, and 1 John 2:17 assures us that "he who does the will of God abides forever." May the Lord be with us!

David said to his son Solomon, "Be strong and of good courage, and do it; do not fear nor be dismayed, for the LORD God—my God—will be with you. He will not leave you nor forsake you."

1 Chronicles 28:20

14

> The beauty of Israel is slain on your high places!
> *How the mighty have fallen!*

"Always speak well of the dead" is an ancient proverb, and David obeyed it when he wrote this elegy in honor of Saul and Jonathan. He says nothing about Saul's selfish and sinful actions, but three times he says, "How the mighty have fallen" (2 Sam. 1:19, 25, 27). Saul was a giant in stature (10:23–24) but a pygmy in character, because he was always hiding.

He hid from accepting responsibility (1 Sam. 10:20–24). Samuel made a dramatic scene out of presenting Israel's first king to the people. He eliminated each tribe until only Benjamin was left, and then he eliminated the clans until only the family of Kish was left. But he couldn't find Saul! He asked the Lord where Saul was, and the Lord said, "There he is, hidden among the equipment" (v. 22), meaning the baggage of the people in the assembly. What was Saul doing there? He had already been anointed by Samuel, so he knew God had chosen him to be king, and there was no reason to hide or even hesitate. Was it a display of fear or false humility? "If God called a man to kingship," G. Campbell Morgan said, "he has no right to hide away." I agree.

He hid from practicing accountability. As you read the life of Saul, you repeatedly see him disobeying God and then making excuses instead of making confession and seeking forgiveness. In 1 Samuel 13, he became impatient as he waited for Samuel to come to offer a sacrifice, so he offered the sacrifice himself and then blamed Samuel because he was "late." In chapter 14, he made a rash oath and blamed his son Jonathan for the consequences—and almost killed him!

In chapter 15, he failed to obey the Lord and kill King Agag and slaughter all the flocks and herds of the enemy. His excuse? The people saved "the best" and destroyed what was worthless. But if God says "Destroy!" there can be no "best"! That excuse cost Saul the kingdom. Saul became paranoid about anybody who assisted David, and he killed all the priestly families in Nob because the high priest had given David and his men some of the sanctuary bread (1 Sam. 21–22). Saul was acting like Satan; he was a liar and a murderer (John 8:44).

He hid from facing reality (1 Sam. 28; 31). Saul was getting no messages from the Lord, which shouldn't have surprised him. "If I regard iniquity in my heart, the Lord will not hear" (Ps. 66:18). The word *regard* means that we know the sin is there, we approve of it, and we plan to do nothing about it. Saul disguised himself and went to consult a witch, for now he got his orders from the devil. However, Saul wasn't disguising himself. He was revealing his true self, for he had been an actor during most of his reign. Samuel told him that the next day would be his last because he and his sons would die in battle (1 Sam. 28:19; 31:1–6). An actor to the very end, Saul led the army even though he knew Israel would lose and he would die.

God never intended for Saul to establish a dynasty, for Israel's king had to come from the tribe of Judah (Gen. 49:10), and David had already been anointed king. Saul's tragic fall reminds me of the words of our Lord in Revelation 3:11, "Behold, I am coming quickly! Hold fast what you have, that no one may take your crown." Saul's career begins with him standing tall (1 Sam. 10:23–24), but it ends with him lying dead. Like Samson, Lot, Judas, and Demas, he did not end well.

Therefore let him who thinks he stands take heed lest he fall.

1 Corinthians 10:12

15

> And David said to Gad, "I am in great distress. Please let us fall into the hand of the LORD, *for His mercies are great*; but do not let me fall into the hand of man."
>
> ━━━━━━━━━━━━━ 2 SAMUEL 24:14

*T*wo sins. Ask a dozen average Bible readers what David's greatest sin was, and most of them will say, "His adultery with Bathsheba." That was indeed a great sin, a sudden, passionate sin of the flesh that caused five deaths—Bathsheba's husband Uriah died, the baby died, and so did three of David's other sons. But when David numbered the people, it was a proud and deliberate sin of the spirit that brought death to seventy thousand people! When David confessed his adultery, he said, "I have sinned against the LORD" (2 Sam. 12:13), but he said "I have sinned greatly" when he confessed the sin of the census. There are sins of the flesh and sins of the spirit (2 Cor. 7:1), and we tend to emphasize the first and minimize the second. But sins of the spirit can also bring terrible consequences. Jesus equated anger with murder and lust with adultery (Matt. 5:21–30). He showed compassion to publicans and sinners, but he called the proud scribes and Pharisees "children of the devil."

Two consequences. God in his government permitted David's sin to bring pain, sorrow, and death, and it hurt David deeply. But God in his grace and mercy forgave David of his sins and even brought good out of great tragedy. Solomon was born to Bathsheba and was made successor to David, and Solomon built the temple on the property David had purchased and on which he had built an altar and sacrificed to God. Only a merciful God can take a man's two heinous sins and build a temple out of them! God is great in mercy

(1 Pet. 1:3) and rich in mercy (Eph. 2:4), and it is much easier to fall into his hands than the hands of others. In Psalm 25:6, David said God's mercies were "tender."

Two thrones. God in his mercy doesn't give us what we *do* deserve and in his grace he gives us what we *don't* deserve— forgiveness! We can come to a throne of *grace* and receive *mercy* (Heb. 4:16). But this doesn't mean we are free to sin as we please because God is merciful and gracious (Rom. 6:1–2)! It simply means that our Father has made provision for us to confess our sins and be forgiven. That's God's grace—but don't forget God's government. Forgiveness is not cheap; it cost Jesus his life. David on his throne was free to disobey God and number the people, but he was not free to change the consequences of his actions.

Two assurances. First, God's mercy never fails. Satan is an accuser (Rev. 12:10) and he seeks to upset us by reminding us of our sins. We must not doubt the promises of God, no matter how we feel when God disciplines us. There may be painful consequences to our sins, but these sorrows don't mean we are not forgiven. God's promise in 1 John 1:9 is true and we must claim it by faith. Second, the prophet Micah wrote the perfect prescription for the heart troubled by memories of sin:

> Who is a God like You,
> Pardoning iniquity
> And passing over the transgression of the remnant of
>   His heritage?
> He does not retain His anger forever,
> Because He delights in mercy.
> He will again have compassion on us,
> And will subdue our iniquities.
> You will cast all our sins
> Into the depths of the sea.
>
> Micah 7:18–19

"And the Lord puts up a sign that says, NO FISHING," as Corrie ten Boom used to say.

16

Now, my God, I pray, let Your eyes be open and let Your ears be attentive to the *prayer made in this place.*

2 CHRONICLES 6:40

Tis place" refers to the temple in Jerusalem, which King Solomon was dedicating that day. The temple was to be "a house of prayer for all nations" (Isa. 56:7; Mark 11:17), and Solomon's prayer set a good example for the people to follow. He emphasized praying *in* the temple when they were in Jerusalem (2 Chron. 6:24, 32, 40) and *toward* the temple when away from home (vv. 20, 21, 26, 34, 38). David prayed toward the temple when he needed the Lord's help (Ps. 28:2; 138:2) and so did the prophet Jonah when he was in the belly of the great fish (Jonah 2:4). The prophet Daniel opened his windows toward Jerusalem when he prayed (Dan. 6:10), and King Jehoshaphat prayed on the battlefield (2 Chron. 18:31–32). If this geographical rule applied to believers today, I would be in real trouble, because I have almost no sense of direction! But all the Lord wants his children to do is lift their hearts heavenward, and in faith say, "Father!"

When we pray in the will of God, we participate in a miracle, because prayer transcends both time and space. *We don't have to worry about geography.* David prayed in a cave (Ps. 57; 142), Paul and Silas prayed in prison (Acts 16:25), King Hezekiah prayed while on his sickbed (Isa. 38), Peter cried out to Jesus while sinking into the Sea of Galilee (Matt. 14:29–33), and Jesus prayed while being nailed to a cross (Luke 23:34). When it comes to praying, Christians need no special equipment, schedule, or environment. If they did, Paul could not have written "pray without ceasing" (1 Thess. 5:17) or "praying always" (Eph. 6:18), and Jesus would never have said that we "always ought to pray and not lose heart" (Luke 18:1).

Prayer is not limited by time, because we are linked to the eternal God who knows the end from the beginning. King Solomon prayed about future situations confronting people yet to be born; and in his prayer recorded in John 17, Jesus prayed for believers who would live in centuries yet to come. *He even prayed for the church today, for you and me* (vv. 20–26). When you come to the throne of grace, ignore calendars, clocks, and maps, and by faith touch the lives and circumstances of people anywhere on planet earth. We don't have to "go to church" to pray. I have prayed in an ambulance as it was hastening me to the hospital after a speeding drunken driver had wrecked my car and almost killed me. I have prayed in a plane that was ditching gas over the Atlantic Ocean. I have prayed in hospital rooms with people whose loved ones were in grave danger. I have prayed while preaching when I sensed the enemy was at work. Claiming Romans 8:28, I have given thanks when everything seemed to be falling apart.

If we stop thinking of prayer as a miracle, our prayer life will start to falter and then cease. We will end up praying so timidly that we're just talking to ourselves instead of to the Lord. Preaching to his London congregation on Sunday morning, October 1, 1882, Charles Haddon Spurgeon said, "However, brethren, whether we like it or not, remember, *asking is the rule of the kingdom*. . . . It is a rule that never will be altered in anybody's case." This reminds us of James 4:2. "Yet you do not have because you do not ask."

"Some people think God does not like to be troubled with our constant coming and asking," D. L. Moody said. "The only way to trouble God is not to come at all."

Are you coming to him and praying?

So I say to you, ask, and it will be given to you; seek, and you will find; knock, and it will be opened to you.

Luke 11:9

> Then Jeshua the son of Jozadak and his brethren the priests, and Zerubbabel the son of Shealtiel and his brethren, *arose and built the altar* of the God of Israel, to offer burnt offerings on it, as it is written in the Law of Moses the man of God.
>
> EZRA 3:2

In 538 BC, about fifty thousand Jewish exiles left Babylon and returned to Jerusalem to rebuild the temple and restore the city. They didn't have an easy life, because the city had been ruined and the enemies of Israel didn't want Jerusalem restored. But the Jews were a united people (Ezra 3:1, 9) and the Lord was with them. Their priorities were right because, without waiting for the temple to be completed, they rebuilt the altar and began to offer the assigned daily sacrifices to the Lord. Here was a new generation making a new beginning as a nation, but they obeyed the instructions from the ancient Law of Moses. They didn't invent anything new; they simply obeyed God's Word. Some believers today need to follow their example.

We have an altar. It's not at the front of a sanctuary on earth but rather enthroned in heaven, for the ascended and exalted Son of God is our altar (Heb. 13:10). It is through him that we offer up our spiritual sacrifices to God (1 Pet. 2:5). I've heard preachers say, "Come to the altar and meet the Lord," but strictly speaking, there are no altars on earth. Jesus has gone through the heavenly veil into the Holy of Holies, and there he intercedes for us (Heb. 6:20). During the Old Testament economy, God met his people at the brazen altar at the door of the tabernacle (Exod. 29:42–43), but today we come to the Father through the Son (John 14:6) and in the Spirit (Eph. 2:18). According to Hebrews 4:14–16, we can come boldly "with freedom of speech" to the throne of grace, present our offerings of worship, and make known our needs. *We have offerings to bring.* Each believer in Jesus Christ is a priest (1 Pet. 2:5, 9; Rev. 1:6) and has the privilege of serving and worshiping God and bringing him "spiritual sacrifices."

The word "spiritual" doesn't mean immaterial, but rather "of a spiritual quality that God can accept." At the start of each day, I must present my body to God as a living sacrifice (Rom. 12:1–2), and I must take time to offer him prayer (Ps. 141:1–3) and praise (Heb. 13:15). During the day I must do good works that honor him (v. 16), and I must use my material resources to help others and glorify God (Phil. 4:14–18; Rom. 15:27). When the local church assembles, it is a "kingdom of priests" bringing spiritual sacrifices to the Lord, and our desire is to please and honor him.

We should bring God our best. Read Malachi 1 where God rebukes the priests for bringing "cheap sacrifices" to the altar. The words of David when he bought the property from Ornan come to mind: "I will surely buy it for the full price, for I will not take what is yours for the LORD, nor offer burnt offerings with that which costs me nothing" (1 Chron. 21:24). What we give and how we give both reveal how much we value our Lord and appreciate his mercies. The word *worship* means "worth-ship," and what we put into our worship shows how much we value the Lord.

Whatever project you are anticipating, be sure you build the altar first. Give to the Lord yourself and all you have and plan to do. Give him the very best. Don't ever give him that which costs you nothing, for worship and service that cost nothing will accomplish nothing.

"When you offer blind animals for sacrifice, is that not wrong? When you sacrifice lame or diseased animals, is that not wrong? . . .With such offerings from your hands, will he accept you?"—says the Lord Almighty.

Malachi 1:8–9 TNIV

18

> The adversaries of Judah . . . came to Zerubbabel
> and the heads of the fathers' houses, and said to
> them, "*Let us build with you.*"

EZRA 4:1-2

A purpose to achieve. It was the Lord who opened the way for the Jewish remnant to return to their land after the Babylonian captivity (2 Chron. 36:22–23). God's salvation plan for the world required that the Jewish nation be restored, the Jewish capital city be repopulated, and the Jewish temple be rebuilt. God made a covenant with Israel and with no other nation on earth, and he will keep that covenant (Gen. 12:1–3; 13:14–17; 17; 22:15–19). There would come a day when the Son of God would be born at Bethlehem, grow up in Nazareth, minister throughout the Holy Land, and finally be crucified outside Jerusalem and put into a tomb. He would rise from the dead, appear to his own followers, and then return to heaven to be enthroned with the Father. "And we have seen and testify that the Father has sent the Son as Savior of the world" (1 John 4:14).

A peril to avoid. Because Israel is God's chosen covenant nation, it is the target of all who reject the Word of God and the Son of God. "So we shall be separate," said Moses to the Lord, "Your people and I, from all the people who are upon the face of the earth" (Exod. 33:16). Israel is "a people dwelling alone, not reckoning itself among the nations" (Num. 23:9). It was the Lord who separated Israel from the other nations (Lev. 20:26) and warned them not to compromise by imitating those nations. If the Jewish builders had accepted the help of these pagan nations, they would have been working with their enemies, and the Lord could not have blessed them. Alas, the Jews did compromise with their

42

pagan neighbors by marrying heathen women (Ezra 10:2). The same principle applies to the church today. "Do not be unequally yoked together with unbelievers," Paul warned, and he went on to explain why (2 Cor. 6:14–7:1). God's people must be separated but not isolated (Eph. 5:8–14).

A promise to affirm. God's unchanging promise to Israel through Abraham says, "I will bless you . . . and you shall be a blessing" (Gen. 12:2). Whenever the nation was out of the will of God and worshiped the gods of the neighboring nations, the people had to endure drought, famine, plagues, and enslavement. Whenever Israel obeyed the terms of the covenant, they were blessed in their families, fields, flocks, and herds, and enjoyed peace in the land. God blessed them and they were a blessing to others. The history of the remnant that returned to the land is not a happy one, for many of the men married heathen wives, and this even included some of the priests (Ezra 9–10). It was important that the Jewish people keep their family tree unpolluted, for the promised Messiah was to be born of a Jewish virgin (Isa. 7:14).

Jesus said, "I will build My church" (Matt. 16:18), and he needs separated, Spirit-filled people to work with him. Christians who compromise with the world are working against him, not with him. "Therefore 'Come out from among them and be separate, says the Lord. Do not touch what is unclean, and I will receive you'" (2 Cor. 6:17). Separation is not isolation, for believers are in this world as salt and light, overcoming decay and darkness (Matt. 5:13–16). That's the kind of people the Lord can use to build his church.

Therefore, having these promises, beloved, let us cleanse ourselves from all filthiness of the flesh and spirit, perfecting holiness in the fear of God.

2 Corinthians 7:1

19

Wherever you hear the sound of the trumpet, rally to us there. Our *God will fight for us.*

Whenever we are faithfully doing God's work, the enemies of God are sure to challenge and attack us. Some professed Christians are upset by the militant imagery in the Bible, but the imagery is there and we can't ignore it. The Jewish people fought many battles during their history, and the church has had its share of conflicts. The first time you find the word *church* in the New Testament, it's connected with building and battling (Matt. 16:18); and the apostle Paul didn't avoid using military metaphors in his letters (Eph. 6:10–20; 2 Tim. 2:1–4; 1 Cor. 15:57; 2 Cor. 2:12–17; 10:4–6). As long as we are fighting God's enemies, God will fight for us.

God's character demands this. "The Lord is a man of war," the women sang after Israel crossed the Red Sea (Exod. 15:3); and when the Amalekites attacked Israel, Moses's prayers and Joshua's army defeated them (17:8–16). Moses memorialized the event by building an altar and calling it "The Lord Is My Banner," definitely a military title. Among the last words of Moses, he describes the Lord as "the shield of your help and the sword of your majesty" (Deut. 33:29). "The Lord shall go forth like a mighty man," wrote Isaiah (42:13), and Jeremiah wrote, "The Lord is with me as a mighty, awesome One" (20:11). Our God is a holy God, and righteousness and justice are evidences of his holy nature. When God's people are fighting against the hosts of wickedness, the Lord is fighting with them.

God's covenant declares this. You will find his covenant with Israel in Leviticus 26–27 and Deuteronomy 28–30. God promised that, when they finally arrived in Canaan, "You will chase your enemies, and they shall fall by the sword before you. Five of you shall chase a hundred, and a hundred of you shall put ten thousand to flight" (Lev. 26:7–8). "The LORD will cause your enemies who rise against you to be defeated before your face; they shall come out against you one way and flee before you seven ways" (Deut. 28:7). The new covenant Jesus made in his blood with his church doesn't include promises relating to land, wealth, and conquest, but spiritually speaking, the principles are the same. Jesus promised that "the gates of Hades shall not prevail against" his church (Matt. 16:18). "Thanks be to God, who gives us the victory through our Lord Jesus Christ" (1 Cor. 15:57). "And this is the victory that has overcome the world—our faith" (1 John 5:4). Christian soldiers wear the shoes of peace (Eph. 6:15), and as we share the gospel, we are waging peace and not war, which is why Satan opposes us. "Yet in all these things we are more than conquerors through Him who loved us" (Rom. 8:37).

God's children must depend on this. In this spiritual warfare, we must do our part by believing the promises of God, being equipped with the armor of God, and being filled with the Spirit of God. This means spending time in the Word daily, surrendering to the Spirit, putting on the armor by faith, and taking our stand for Christ. Double-minded Christian soldiers become victims, not victors. As the old hymn puts it, "Stand up, stand up for Jesus!" Witnessing about Jesus goes hand-in-hand with spiritual warfare, and battles give us some of our best opportunities for sharing the Gospel.

When the battles come, remember what Nehemiah said: "God will fight for us." You are not fighting alone. But God doesn't fight instead of us, because we have our part to do.

Fight the good fight of faith.
1 Timothy 6:12

20

Then we departed from the river of Ahava on the twelfth day of the first month, to go to Jerusalem. And *the hand of our God* was upon us, and He delivered us from the hand of the enemy and from ambush along the road.

EZRA 8:31

I f you can explain what's going on in your life and ministry, then God didn't do it; so be sure to keep your life on a miracle basis." Dr. Bob Cook, then president of Youth for Christ, said that at a YFC conference many years ago and I've never forgotten it. Without God's hand upon his people, we could never experience God's power and make progress in our Christian walk and work. If any book in the Bible illustrates this truth, it's the book of Ezra. "The hand of God" was at work for his people in wonderful ways.

The hand of God directs us. "The king's heart is in the hand of the LORD, like the rivers of water; He turns it wherever He wishes" (Prov. 21:1). The prophet Jeremiah had predicted that the Jews would be exiles in Babylon for seventy years and then permitted to return to their land (Jer. 25:1–14; 29:10–11). The exiled prophet Daniel understood this fact, and he claimed God's promise and devoted himself to prayer (Dan. 9). The heart of King Cyrus was moved by the Lord and he set the exiles free (Ezra 1:1–4). Their liberty came, not by political pressure, demonstrations, or bribes, but by God's people believing God's promises and praying.

The king's heart was moved by the hand of the Lord and so were the hearts of the Jewish exiles who decided to return to their land (Ezra 1:5). About fifty thousand of them left Babylon and made the long journey to Jerusalem. During their years of exile, many families had become comfortable and preferred to remain in Babylon, but the dedicated remnant stepped out by faith to return to their land and rebuild their temple. The Jews who remained gave generously of their wealth, and King Cyrus returned to the priests the furnishings they would need for the ministry in the temple (vv. 5–8). Only God could get the glory for these remarkable events. We would experience more such events today if we gave ourselves to the Word and prayer (Acts 6:4).

The hand of God protects us. In these days of rapid communication and transportation, we think nothing of making long journeys; but in ancient days, the picture was not so bright. Travel was dangerous, for bands of thieves watched the roads for caravans, and it was also uncomfortable and tiring, but the hand of the Lord protected his people. When the people reached Jerusalem, they found themselves surrounded by enemies who did not want Jerusalem rebuilt, and the Lord gave the Jews the insight and courage not to compromise. Satan starts his attack by being a serpent that deceives (Ezra 4:1–5) and if that fails, then he comes as a lion that devours. But the hand of God is powerful and gives us victory.

The hand of God corrects us. Ezra 9–10 and Nehemiah 9–13 tell the sad tale of the Jewish men disobeying God's law and taking pagan wives. If the leaders had allowed this compromise to continue, it would have polluted the nation's "godly seed" (Mal. 2:13–16). The leaders had to exercise discipline, for "whom the LORD loves, He chastens" (Heb. 12:5–6). If we obey the Lord, his hand will pour out blessing; but if we rebel, his hand will be heavy upon us (Ps. 32:3). May the good hand of the Lord always be upon us as we seek to serve him!

The right hand of the LORD is exalted;
The right hand of the LORD does valiantly.

Psalm 118:16

So the wall was finished on the twenty-fifth day of Elul, in fifty-two days.

NEHEMIAH 6:15

Beginning a project is one thing; bringing it to a successful conclusion is quite something else. Nehemiah and his fellow-workers ended their work successfully and Jerusalem was protected by strong gates and walls. The enemy had laughed at the Jews and said it couldn't be done, but it *was* done—and done well. One of the important things about this project is the balance it displays, the kind of balance that is needed in every work we do for the Lord.

Leading and following. It all began when Nehemiah's heart was broken after hearing his brother's report that Jerusalem was in a shameful mess and the object of ridicule by the Gentile neighbors (Neh. 1). Nehemiah wept and prayed and asked God to help him do something about the matter, and God answered his prayer. With the king's permission, he left the comfortable palace, traveled to Jerusalem, surveyed the situation, and shared his burden with the elders of his people. The word *leaders* is mentioned eight times in chapter 3, indicating that the city was organized, and Nehemiah further organized the work crews. A great vision must be accompanied by careful supervision if you want to avoid derision. Chapter 3 reveals that not everybody volunteered to work (v. 5), and that the workforce included priests (v. 1), skilled craftsmen (vv. 8, 32), women (v. 12), and even people from outside Jerusalem (vv. 2, 5, 7). Some people did more work than others (vv. 11, 19, 21, 24, 27, 30).

Building and battling (Neh. 4:18). In the Christian life, building and battling go together (Luke 14:25–33); for if we aren't armed, how can we defend what we have built? Our war equipment is described in Ephesians 6:10–20, and we put it on by faith each day. Spiritually speaking, our tools are the Word of God and prayer. We must always be on guard lest we lose what we have gained (2 John 8), or lest we are so involved in fighting that we forget to build! God's warriors and workers must be balanced.

Watching and praying (Neh. 4:9). Working, watching (staying alert), praying, and battling would be a challenge to anybody! The phrase "watch and pray" is found in Mark 13:33 and 14:38, Ephesians 6:18, and Colossians 4:2–4, texts that are worth pondering. There are so many distractions in today's world that it's becoming more and more difficult to focus on being alert and actively doing our work. Being alert means staying awake. Peter, James, and John went to sleep on the Mount of Transfiguration (Luke 9:32) and in the Garden of Gethsemane (Luke 22:45). Sleeping saints are victims, not victors!

Believing and serving (James 2:14–26). It isn't enough for us only to pray for our ministry; we must also minister. "For as the body without the spirit is dead, so faith without works is dead also" (James 2:26). Nehemiah and his workers beautifully illustrate the balance we need if we are to be effective servants of the Lord. If our faith is genuine, it will motivate us to do the work God has equipped us to do. Nehemiah believed that God wanted the walls rebuilt and the gates repaired and re-hung, and that he was the one to lead the project. God's calling is God's enabling, and our responsibility is to "trust and obey."

A friend of mine, now in glory, often said, "Blessed are the balanced." I recommend that beatitude to you.

[Remember] without ceasing your work of faith, labor of love, and patience of hope in our Lord Jesus Christ in the sight of our God and Father.

1 Thessalonians 1:3

22

> You are just in all that has befallen us; *for You have dealt faithfully*, but we have done wickedly.

NEHEMIAH 9:33

This psalm was sung by the Jews at the Feast of Tabernacles after the walls of Jerusalem had been completed. The people confessed their sins and rededicated themselves to God. The psalm magnifies many of the attributes of God, but we want to emphasize his faithfulness.

We have a faithful Creator (1 Pet. 4:19). Peter wrote this letter to prepare the believers in the Roman Empire for the persecution, the "fiery trial" that was soon to occur (vv. 12–19). As never before, they had to commit themselves to the Lord who is a "faithful Creator." If he can create and sustain a universe such as ours, he can surely take care of his people and meet their needs. When circumstances upset you, turn to your faithful Creator and let him take charge.

We have a faithful High Priest (Heb. 2:17–18). Jesus ministers today in heaven as both King and Priest, and he is able to give us the grace we need whenever we are tempted or tested (4:14–16). The child of God should never say, "Nobody knows how I feel!" because Jesus understands us perfectly, knows our needs, and sympathizes with us. When he was here on earth, he experienced every test and temptation that we might experience today, and he alone can give us the grace we need to triumph over our enemies.

We have a faithful Advocate (1 John 1:9–2:1). But what if we don't turn to the Lord for the grace that we need? What if we listen to the enemy and disobey the Lord? Then Satan accuses us and tells us what failures we are, and that just makes matters worse. But Jesus does not forsake us! He died for all our sins and is our advocate before the throne of God. When we confess our sins, he is faithful to keep his promise and forgive us. He has already died for all our sins and the Father graciously forgives when his children confess their sins. Read Zechariah 3 for an illustration of this experience—and believe it.

We have a faithful Witness (Rev. 1:5; 3:14). When he was ministering on earth, Jesus clearly spoke the Word of God, and his words are recorded in the Scriptures. "What He has seen and heard, that He testifies," John the Baptist said. "For He whom God has sent speaks the words of God, for God does not give the Spirit by measure" (John 3:32, 34; *see* John 18:37). The Spirit of God enables us to understand and apply the Word to our own lives, and this is the way we "grow in the grace and knowledge of our Lord and Savior Jesus Christ" (2 Pet. 3:18).

We have a faithful Conqueror (Rev. 19:11). Yes, Jesus is the Prince of Peace, but he is also the Conqueror who will defeat every enemy and establish his kingdom (2 Thess. 1:7–10). Believers today are "more than conquerors through him who loved us" (Rom. 8:37). One day the Lamb will come in his wrath as the Lion, and he will be wearing the name "KING OF KINGS AND LORD OF LORDS" (Rev. 19:16). Let's let him win the battles for us today!

The Lord is faithful, so let's trust in him and not in ourselves. We are not victors because we put faith in our own faith but because we put faith in Christ who always deals with us faithfully. How do we get our faith strengthened? Pioneer missionary to China J. Hudson Taylor wrote, "Not by striving after faith, but by resting on the Faithful One." He pointed to 2 Timothy 2:13, "If we are faithless, He remains faithful." Rest in the Faithful One!

> His compassions fail not.
> They are new every morning.
> Great is Your faithfulness.
>
> Lamentations 3:22–23

23

> Since his days are determined, the number of his months is with You; *You have appointed his limits*, so that he cannot pass.

JOB 14:5

To be human is to accept the limitations that God in his wisdom has imposed upon us and upon the world into which he has placed us. God has limited the seas (Job 38:10–11), he has limited Satan (1:12; 2:6), and he draws the boundaries of the nations (Acts 17:26). Even our first parents in paradise were limited in what they could do, and because they overstepped the limits, they were cast out (Gen. 3). Individually, you and I are limited in our abilities, our opportunities, our resources, and even the length of our life. God has appointed the limits. Our days are numbered and we cannot go beyond that final day, although we may foolishly hasten it. As far as the law is concerned, all people are created equal, but as far as life is concerned, we are unequal, because human life involves individual limitations.

But limitations give us freedoms. I have met the conditions for securing a driver's license and this gives me the freedom to drive on the public streets and highways. My wife and I have met the conditions for possessing passports and this gave us the freedom to travel the world and minister. The Bible gives us the conditions we must meet if we want to receive answers to prayer, and if we obey, God will grant what we request. This is one of the differences between freedom and license. True freedom isn't doing what I always want to do but what God wants me to do, and my obedience opens the way to blessing.

We must move a step further: *true freedom encourages cooperation*. Because my abilities and possessions are limited, there are many things I don't know and can't do. Therefore, I need the help of others. God saw that Adam's loneliness was not good, so he created a mate for him to help compensate for his own limitations (Gen. 2:18–25). Marriage, family, and friends are gifts from the heart of God to help us function in this world of limitations, for we can all help one another. The family, community, and church are similar: we belong to each other, we affect each other, and we need each other.

Life involves limitations, limitations give us freedoms, freedoms result in cooperation, and *cooperation makes us serious about life*. When our lives are connected with others in love, those others become special to us and we don't want to lose them. "So teach us to number our days, that we may gain a heart of wisdom" (Ps. 90:12). God has set a limit to our days, but we don't know what it is. God has written all our days in his book, but we haven't seen the pages (139:15–16).

The conclusion of the matter is this: we must value our lives and the lives of others, for they are limited. We must know that God has appointed our limits, especially our lifespan. We must make the best possible use of the hours and days God gives us, which means knowing and doing his will. Jesus said, "I must work the works of Him who sent me while it is day; the night is coming when no one can work" (John 9:4). Our limitations are not obstacles; they are opportunities. God has appointed our limitations so we will focus on what he wants us to do. As the old saying expresses it: "I cannot do everything, but I can do something. I must do what I can do as long as God enables me, and I must be faithful until he instructs me otherwise."

See then that you walk circumspectly, not as fools but as wise, redeeming the time, because the days are evil.

Ephesians 5:15–16

> I have uttered what I did not understand, *things too wonderful for me*, which I did not know.
>
> ══════════════════════ JOB 42:3

There are more than ten thousand words in the book of Job, most of them spoken by God, Job, and Job's four visitors. Job was an exemplary believer, but Satan argued that Job obeyed God only because God blessed him. God permitted Satan to take from Job his wealth, his health, and his ten children, leaving him sitting on the ash heap outside the city, trying to alleviate his sorrow and pain. For many days, Job and his visitors argued back and forth, trying to explain the ways of God; but they reached no valid conclusion. However, there are three "silences" in the book that are very revealing and helpful to us today.

The silence of sympathy (Job 2:11–13). Job's friends traveled long distances to reach him, and when they arrived, the sight of Job greatly distressed them. It made them weep, tear their clothes, throw dust into the air, and then sit in silence for an entire week, for "they saw that his grief was very great" (2:13). They knew that the best way to identify with his pain was just to say nothing. Job had no words to express his feelings and they had no words to comfort him. There are words that heal but there are also silences that heal, and there are silences that speak clearer and better than words.

The silence of authority (chaps. 3–37). As you read the speeches of the four visitors, you wonder why the Lord didn't exercise his divine authority, interrupt them, and straighten them out. Instead, he kept quiet. There are 329 questions asked in the book of Job, yet there are not many answers. Each man thought he was on the right track, but all of them were confused. Zophar's questions in 11:7–8 should have jolted them:

"Can you search out the deep things of God? Can you find out the limits of the Almighty? They are higher than heaven—what can you do? Deeper than Sheol—what can you know?" No matter how much we think we know, Paul makes it clear that "we know in part" (1 Cor. 13:9). If we don't have all the parts, we can't assemble the puzzle, no matter how dogmatic we are. The Lord's silence during this discussion allowed the men to use words to obscure truth and ignore action. While intelligent discussions have their part in life, words are not substitutes for deeds. The fact that politicians and leaders make speeches doesn't mean they are solving problems with their words. Sometimes they make the problems worse! Novelist Joseph Conrad wrote, "Words are the great foes of reality." Ponder that.

The silence of discovery (Job 42:1–6). Job listened to what God had to say and learned more about himself than he ever expected to know. He had been "darken[ing] counsel by words without knowledge" (38:2) and demanding that God come to him and allow him to defend himself. But when the Lord showed up, Job was speechless and laid his hand over his mouth (40:3–5). When God finished the interrogation, Job had to confess that he had uttered words he didn't understand! Once he had seen God and seen himself, the only thing he could do was repent. Then God refuted the visitors and vindicated Job. King David had experienced a similar awakening (Ps. 131).

In today's noisy and talkative world, we must find time for the ministry of silence if we hope to hear the still small voice of God. Yes, we need to watch our words, but we also need to watch our silences. Otherwise, how else can we know ourselves and the Lord?

And behold, the LORD passed by, and a great and strong wind tore into the mountains and broke the rocks in pieces before the LORD, but the LORD was not in the wind; and after the wind an earthquake, but the LORD was not in the earthquake; and after the earthquake a fire, but the LORD was not in the fire; and after the fire a still small voice.

1 Kings 19:11–12

25

Keep me as the apple of Your eye; hide me under
the shadow of your wings.

PSALM 17:8

These are not the wings of the hen protecting her chicks (Matt. 23:37), but the wings of the cherubim in the Holy of Holies of the sanctuary (Exod. 25:10–22). No one but the high priest could enter the Holy of Holies, and he could enter only once a year on the Day of Atonement (Lev. 16). He sprinkled the blood of the sacrifice on the mercy seat, under the wings of the two cherubim. This imagery is mentioned eight times in Scripture. As you read Psalm 17, note that David tells us what God does for those who live under his wings: he saves, he keeps, and he satisfies.

He saves (Ps. 17:7). We need to be saved because we have broken God's law and deserve judgment. The mercy seat with the cherubim was the covering for the ark, and in the ark were the tablets of the law. Israel had broken the law, and so have we; and "it is the blood that makes atonement for the soul" (Lev. 17:11). The priest sprinkled the blood on the mercy seat, and when God looked down, he didn't see the broken law. He saw only the atoning blood. When Jesus Christ died on the cross, his blood paid the price of our salvation. "In Him we have redemption through His blood, the forgiveness of sins, according to the riches of His grace" (Eph. 1:7). Ruth of Moab was outside the covenant blessings of Israel until she put her faith in Jehovah, the true and living God (Ruth 1:16–17). The result? "The LORD repay your work, and a full reward be given you by the LORD God of Israel, under whose wings you have come for refuge" (2:12).

He keeps (Ps. 17:8). "Be merciful to me, O God, be merciful to me! For my soul trusts in You; and in the shadow of

56

Your wings I will make my refuge, until these calamities have passed by" (57:1). David's life was in danger when he wrote that, and he was hiding in a cave, but his faith was in God alone. Psalm 61 is a similar prayer, and David wrote, "I will abide in Your tabernacle forever; I will trust in the shelter of Your wings" (v. 4). The safest place for the people of God is in the Holy of Holies, overshadowed by the Lord. "He who dwells in the secret place of the Most High shall abide under the shadow of the Almighty" (91:1). This is the Old Testament version of John 15:4, "Abide in Me, and I in you."

He satisfies (Ps. 17:15). "Therefore the children of men put their trust under the shadow of Your wings. They are abundantly satisfied with the fullness of Your house, and You give them drink from the river of Your pleasures" (36:7–8). "Because You have been my help, therefore in the shadow of Your wings I will rejoice" (63:7). What a life! Joyful satisfaction, abundance, fullness and pleasure, all from the heart of God! "My soul shall be satisfied" (v. 5).

In the Old Testament, the law established boundaries (Exod. 21:12, 19–21) and warned people not to get too near the holy ground, but the grace of God takes down the walls (Eph. 2:14), rends the veil (Matt. 27:51), and invites us to get closer to the Lord. "Draw near to God and He will draw near to you" (James 4:8). "Therefore, brethren, having boldness to enter the Holiest by the blood of Jesus . . . and having a high priest over the house of God, let us draw near" (Heb. 10:19, 21–22). Because we are "under his wings," we have salvation, security, and satisfaction.

There is therefore now no condemnation to those who are in Christ Jesus.

Romans 8:1

26

The LORD *is my shepherd*; I shall not want.

When he wrote those words, now so familiar to us, David was boldly making several declarations about himself and everyone who has put saving faith in Jesus Christ.

If we honestly can say, "The Lord is my shepherd," then *we truly are his sheep*. Before we trusted Christ, we were *lost* sheep. "All we like sheep have gone astray; we have turned, every one, to his own way; and the LORD has laid on Him the iniquity of us all" (Isa. 53:6). Now that Jesus has found us and made us part of his flock, he alone is our shepherd. It may embarrass some Christians to be called sheep, because sheep are almost defenseless, they have poor eyesight, and they are prone to wander. However, the Bible doesn't compare us to steeds or lions, but to sheep, and that's why we need a shepherd. "O LORD, I know the way of man is not in himself; it is not in man who walks to direct his own steps" (Jer. 10:23). Have you discovered that fact?

If Jesus is our shepherd, then *we listen to his voice*. Three times in John 10, Jesus says that his sheep hear his voice (vv. 3, 16, 27). They not only know (recognize) his voice (v. 4) but they also recognize and ignore the voices of false teachers who deny Christ (v. 5). The voice of the Good Shepherd is the Word of God, and the Holy Spirit enables the sheep to discern God's truth in a world filled with error (1 John 4:1–6). If the Lord is truly your shepherd, you will spend time daily reading the Word and meditating on the truth as it is in Jesus (Eph. 4:21).

If Jesus is our shepherd, then *we will follow him*. The sheep follow Jesus because "they know his voice" (John 10:4). It isn't enough simply to read the Word; we must obey what it says. The Good Shepherd feeds us and leads us by his Word. Spiritual maturity comes, not from the routine reading of the Bible or religious books, but from inwardly "digesting" and outwardly obeying the Word of God. "Be doers of the word, and not hearers only, deceiving yourselves" (James 1:22). Psalm 23 makes it clear that we must follow Jesus or we will miss everything he has planned for us day by day: the green pastures, the still waters, the fellowship of the flock, protection as we go through the valley or into the fold at night, fellowship at the table, the anointing to refresh us, and so much more.

If Jesus is our shepherd, then *we should be profitable to him*. The flocks provided the shepherds and their families with milk, fleece, meat, lambs, and also with sacrifices for the annual feasts or for special worship. Jewish shepherds did not aimlessly slaughter their sheep because the animals were too valuable, but they did give their best to be offered to the Lord. God's people are to be "living" sacrifices (Rom. 12:1–2), wholly yielded to him. We are to "reproduce" as we share the gospel and bring others to the Savior. When we consider the price Jesus paid to make us his sheep, we ought to want to give our all, our best, to him.

Finally, if we are truly his sheep, *we know we are going to heaven*. "I will dwell in the house of the LORD forever" (Ps. 23:6). "In My Father's house are many mansions," Jesus said. "I go to prepare a place for you" (John 14:1–3). When we get to heaven, the Shepherd will still care for us.

It isn't sufficient to say "The Lord is a shepherd" or "The Lord is the shepherd." We must say from our hearts, "The Lord is *my* shepherd." He calls his people "My sheep" because he purchased us with his blood, and we call him "My shepherd" because we have trusted him.

The Lamb who is in the midst of the throne will shepherd them and lead them to living fountains of waters. And God will wipe away every tear from their eyes.

Revelation 7:17

27

> The counsel of the LORD stands forever, *the plans of His heart* to all generations.
>
> **PSALM 33:11**

You and I should have no problems with the first half of our verse, because we know that our heavenly Father is sovereign and that his counsel will ultimately triumph. But when it comes to the second half, some believers might hesitate, and you may be one of them. You may have had painful experiences in your Christian life that make it difficult for you to believe that the will of God comes from the heart of God and is an expression of his love. If the Father loves us, why is there so much disappointment, pain, and sorrow in life? When what we consider to be "bad things" do happen to God's people, these are times when the enemy asks us, "If God loves you, why did this happen?" How do we deal with these difficult experiences?

Accept God's overall purpose. The Father's wise counsel for all of his children is that we become "conformed to the image of His Son" (Rom. 8:29). The trials of life are tools in God's hands to make us more like Jesus, and whether we see it or not, all things *are* working together for good (v. 28). But the Father also has purposes for us *individually.* He admonishes each of us to work out our own salvation, our Christian life, with fear and trembling as he works in us (Phil. 2:12–13). Joseph couldn't fully understand why he was suffering so much, but it all worked together to put him on the throne and make him more like Jesus. The twelve disciples didn't understand why their Master should suffer and die, but they finally got the message.

Submit to God's daily plans. "There are many plans in a man's heart, nevertheless the LORD's counsel—that will stand" (Prov. 19:21). Many times in my life and ministry I have turned to Jeremiah 29:11 and found encouragement: "For I know the thoughts that I think toward you, says the LORD, thoughts of peace and not of evil, to give you a future and a hope." God has a whole universe to manage, and the fact that he thinks about us at all is an encouragement in itself. If we trust him, his plans for us will enlarge our hope and lead to a bright future. This promise reminds me of the family in Bethany and the trials they experienced. John 11:5 says, "Now Jesus loved Martha and her sister and Lazarus." If so, why did Jesus allow Lazarus to get sick and then die? And why did he delay in going to Bethany to help the two sisters he loved? But it all worked together to bring glory to God. "My times are in Your hand" (Ps. 31:15).

Rest in God's love. Whether for Mary, Martha, and Lazarus or for you and me, the will of God does come from the heart of God and manifests his love for us. When our older son was in first grade, he tried to climb a picket fence and severely injured himself. As we drove to the clinic, he was frightened and worried and asked me, "What will the doctor do?" I explained that the doctor would sterilize the wound and give him a tetanus shot, and probably a few stitches, all of which would be painful. But all of it would work together to heal him. Why was I taking him to the doctor? Because his mother and I loved him and wanted the best for him. My heavenly Father did not spare his own son whom he loved (Rom. 8:32), and he will not spare us. The Father forsook his own Son *so that he might never forsake us!* No matter how we feel, the Lord by his grace can transform suffering into glory and make us more like his Son.

> You will guide me with Your counsel,
> and afterward receive me to glory.
>
> Psalm 73:24

> A man's heart plans his way,
> But the LORD directs his steps.
>
> Proverbs 16:9

28

> *My soul thirsts for God*, for the living God. When
> shall I come and appear before God?

PSALM 42:2

The first three verses of Psalm 42 mention the essentials of physical life: air (v. 1), water (v. 2), and food (v. 3). Spiritually speaking, air, water, and food are essential to a healthy spiritual life. The Spirit of God is our breath (John 20:22) and our water (7:37–39), and the Word of God is our food (Matt. 4:4). Air, water, and food are necessities, not luxuries. In this meditation, I want to focus on water for drinking, which is a symbol of the Holy Spirit. (Water for washing is a symbol of the Word of God. *See* John 15:3 and Eph. 5:26.) What is involved in this important experience of "spiritual thirsting"?

Thirst involves desiring. People who claim to be Christian should have a keen desire to know God better and want to fellowship more intimately with him. If that thirst is lacking, the person is either not a believer at all or is a believer who is drinking at the wrong fountains. "For My people have committed two evils: they have forsaken Me, the fountain of living waters, and hewn themselves cisterns—broken cisterns that can hold no water" (Jer. 2:13). It's a dangerous thing to live on substitutes. "You have made us for yourself," wrote St. Augustine, "and our hearts are restless until they rest in you." An idol is a substitute for God, and substitutes cannot impart real life. After describing in Psalm 115 the sad characteristics of dead idols, the psalmist writes, "Those who make them are like them; so is everyone who trusts in them" (v. 8). Do we have a deep desire to know God and become more like him? "O God, You are my God; early will I seek You; my soul thirsts for You" (63:1). That is reality!

Thirst involves deciding. "What will you have to drink?" asks the server in the restaurant, and we must make a decision. But when it comes to spiritual thirst, there can be only one choice for the dedicated believer: "The Spirit and the bride say, 'Come!' And let him who hears say, 'Come!' And let him who thirsts come. Whoever desires, let him take the water of life freely" (Rev. 22:17). When my doctor told me I was diabetic, he gave me a great piece of advice: "Lose your appetite for the things that aren't good for you." *You make the decisions! Change your appetite!* The invitation is quite simple: come—take—drink. "If anyone thirsts, let him come to Me and drink" (John 7:37). It's an act of faith that leads to the kind of heart satisfaction that nothing in the world can replace.

Thirst involves delighting. People who advertise foods, beverages, and other items of personal consumption often stress "satisfaction." But if these products really satisfied, *the consumers would never purchase another one!* Jesus does satisfy us in every way and we have no desire to replace him. "Whoever drinks of the water that I shall give him will never thirst," Jesus said (John 4:14). Unsaved people spend a lifetime thirsting for satisfaction and then die and spend eternity unable to quench their thirst (Luke 16:19–31). Like the river in Ezekiel 47:1–12, the river of the water of life gets deeper and deeper for the child of God.

The water of life is free for the taking, but it cost Jesus his life to make it available to us. He thirsted on the cross that we might never thirst (John 19:28). That invitation has never been cancelled. Have you answered it? If you have, are you sharing the invitation with others?

I will give of the fountain of the water of life freely to him who thirsts.

Revelation 21:6

63

29

> *God reigns over the nations*; God sits on His holy throne.

PSALM 47:8

The patriarchs, psalmists, prophets, and apostles never heard the word *globalization*, but they still had an interest in the nations of the world. Jehovah wasn't a local Jewish deity; he was and is "ruler over the kings of the earth" (Rev. 1:5). In God's eyes, the nations are "as a drop in the bucket . . . as the small dust on the scales" (Isa. 40:15), but they are also the fields into which the church sows the seed of the Word of God (Matt. 28:18–20). God's ministries to the nations are important to every Christian believer who prays "Your kingdom come."

God made the nations. "And He has made of one blood every nation of men to dwell on all the face of the earth" (Acts 17:26). The nations began with Adam and Eve and developed after the flood (Gen. 10–11), and then spread abroad. While the focus of the Old Testament is primarily on Israel, dozens of other nations are mentioned, and Christ's "Great Commission" exhorts us to take the gospel to every nation (Luke 24:46–49). God made the nations.

God sustains the nations, "for in Him we live and move and have our being" (Acts 17:28). While nations have different languages, customs, and resources, they all depend on the sunshine, rain, food, wind, and soil provided by the Lord. They also depend on one another. I understand that our telephones contain materials from at least twenty-two different nations. This is where globalization comes in.

God assigns their times and borders. He has "determined their preappointed times and the boundaries of their dwellings" (Acts 17:26). Nations and empires come and go and national borders change, but national history and geography are in the hands of God. The Lord also has a hand in the leaders of the nations. "He removes kings and raises up kings" (Dan. 2:21). "The Most High rules in the kingdom of men, and gives it to whomever He chooses" (Dan. 4:32). "God is the Judge: He puts down one, and exalts another" (Ps. 75:7). This doesn't mean that God is to blame for the foolish and selfish things leaders have done, for each one of us is accountable to God for our own decisions. God can even use unconverted government leaders to fulfill his will. He used the Gentile nations to chasten his people Israel and a Roman emperor to make sure Jesus would be born in Bethlehem.

God desires that the nations be saved, "so that they should seek the Lord . . . and find Him, though He is not far from each one of us" (Acts 17:27). In Old Testament times, Israel was called to be a "light to the Gentiles" (Isa. 42:6; 49:6) but failed in that ministry. Through the witness of the church today, that light must go into all the world (Luke 2:32; Acts 13:42–47). The nations have rebelled against the Lord (Ps. 2:1–3), but his invitation still goes forth to Jews and Gentiles alike (Ps. 2:10–12).

We who know the Lord must remember that, by his grace, he has "raised us up together, and made us sit together" with Christ (Eph. 2:5–6). He has made us kings (Rev. 1:5–6) and we can "reign in life through the One, Jesus Christ" (Rom. 5:17). When God ushers in the new heaven and the new earth, God's people shall reign with him forever and ever (Rev. 22:3–5).

Don't forget to pray for the lost in the nations of the world and to do all you can to share the gospel with them. God wants to redeem people "out of every tribe and tongue and people and nation" (Rev. 5:9). God reigns over every nation; is he reigning over our lives?

> God reigns over the nations;
> God sits on His holy throne.
>
> Psalm 47:8

65

30

As we have heard, so we have seen in the city of the LORD of hosts, in the city of our God: *God will establish it forever.*

PSALM 48:8

As time marches on, empires, nations, and cities and their famous leaders come and go, but the city of Jerusalem will be established forever! No other city can claim that distinction. You find Jerusalem mentioned over eight hundred times in Scripture, beginning at Genesis 14:18 ("Salem," which means *peace*; *see* Heb. 7:1–10) and ending at Revelation 21:10. What kind of a city is Jerusalem?

A chosen city. Salvation history is wrapped up in a number of choices that God made in his gracious and sovereign will. First, out of all the heavenly bodies he created, the Lord chose the earth to be the place where his plan would be worked out (Ps. 24:1). Out of all the peoples on earth, he chose the Jews to bring the Word of God and the Son of God into the world (Deut. 7:6), for "salvation is of the Jews" (John 4:22). He chose Canaan to be the homeland of his people Israel (Deut. 1:8), and he chose Mt. Zion to be the location of the capital city of the nation. Jerusalem would also be the home of the sanctuary in which the Lord would dwell (Ps. 132:13–18). Jerusalem is his chosen city (Zech. 3:2) and David was his chosen king to establish the dynasty that would bring Jesus Christ into the world (1 Kings 11:34). What a city!

A guilty city. Jerusalem is "the holy city" (Neh. 11:1, 18; Isa. 48:2; Matt. 4:5; 27:53) and "the city of God" (Ps. 46:4; 48:1; Isa. 60:14). The ancient Jewish people were proud of their city and called it "the perfection of beauty, the joy of all the earth" (Lam. 2:15). But when the Son of God, Jesus Christ, came to earth, he found the city defiled and in bondage, and he wept over the guilty city (Matt. 23:25–39; Luke 13:34–35).

A heavenly city (Heb. 12:18–24). The Christian's "Mount Zion" is not on earth in the Holy Land but in heaven. Our Father and our Savior are in heaven, and our home and destiny are also there. Our treasures should be there also (Matt. 6:19–21). Galatians 4:21–32 explains that Christians belong to "the Jerusalem above," for God's children are all citizens of heaven (Phil. 3:20). Like the patriarchs of old, we are pilgrims and strangers on this earth, and we are looking for our permanent home in heaven (Heb. 11:13–16). We should "seek those things which are above, where Christ is" and set our minds "on things above, not on things on the earth" (Col. 3:1–2). Everything we need ultimately must come from God. In Psalm 87, the sons of Korah wrote about the earthly Zion, but we can apply what they wrote to our heavenly Zion and say, "All my springs are in you" (v. 7). Jesus invites us to come to him and drink (John 7:37–39).

An eternal city. One day, there will be a new heaven and a new earth, and a new Jerusalem will descend to earth from God (Rev. 21:1–6). This will be the fulfillment of Psalm 48:8, "God will establish [Jerusalem] forever." The last two chapters of Revelation describe the greatness and the glory of the city. The glorified children of God will have homes in heaven and access to the heavenly city on the new earth! Believing Jews and Gentiles will be united in that city, for the twelve gates are named after the tribes of Israel and the twelve foundations after the apostles (Rev. 21:9–15). "I go to prepare a place for you," Jesus said (John 14:1–3).

I recall hearing a television anchorman say, "Jerusalem is the key to peace in the middle east." I thought of Psalm 122:6, "Pray for the peace of Jerusalem."

Are you praying?

Brethren, my heart's desire and prayer to God for Israel is that they may be saved.

Romans 10:1

31

> Wash me thoroughly from my iniquity, and *cleanse me from my sin.*

PSALM 51:2

I once asked radio Bible teacher Theodore Epp what counsel he gave to unfaithful married couples who wanted to make a new beginning, and he replied, "I tell them to take a good bath in Psalm 51!" When it comes to confessing sin, David does set a good example for us.

He was accountable. You don't find David saying "we" or "they" but rather "I," "me," and "my." It's "my iniquity . . . my transgressions . . . my sin." Unlike Adam and Eve, or his predecessor King Saul, David didn't try to blame somebody else. At first, he had schemed in his attempt to hide his sins, but such schemes are not successful. "He who covers his sins will not prosper" (Prov. 28:13). With the words of the prophet Nathan, God stabbed David in the heart—"You are the man" (2 Sam. 12:7). The person who doesn't take repentance seriously does not take sin seriously. "If we say that we have not sinned, we make Him a liar, and His word is not in us" (1 John 1:10). Our sins are serious; they put Jesus on the cross.

He was burdened and broken. Psalm 51 is not the flippant prayer of an immature child but the tear-drenched confession of an adult servant of God who was deeply sorry for his sins. David had lost his purity and damaged his integrity and now he pleaded for the Lord to restore his joy (v. 12). He had transgressed God's law and rebelled against him. It used to be that, wherever David looked, he saw some blessing from God to sing about; but now, wherever he looked, he saw only his sins (v. 3). This doesn't mean we must manufacture tears and dramatic emotions in order for the Lord to forgive us, but it does mean that we are to be truly sorry for what we did. "A broken and a contrite heart—these, O God, You will not despise" (v. 17). God dwells with the believer "who has a contrite and humble spirit" (Isa. 57:15).

He was confident. We don't hear David trying to make bargains with God. From the very beginning, David depended on the character of God, on his mercy and his lovingkindness (Ps. 51:1). David knew he could trust the promises of God. The king was required to read the book of the Law faithfully, so David must have known what the Lord had said to Moses in Exodus: "The LORD, the LORD God, merciful and gracious, longsuffering, and abounding in goodness and truth, keeping mercy for thousands, forgiving iniquity and transgression and sin" (Exod. 34:6–7). Later in life, David said, "Please let us fall into the hands of the LORD, for His mercies are great" (2 Sam. 24:14). Believers today rest on 1 John 1:9.

He dedicated himself to serve (Ps. 51:13, 18–19). Until he was forgiven, David was in no condition to minister to anyone else; but once he was cleansed, God could use him. His service and his worship would then be acceptable to God. He could witness to sinners and tell them of the forgiveness of the Lord, and he could go to the sanctuary and sing to the Lord. He could encourage the men repairing the walls of Jerusalem and the priests offering sacrifices. His prayer in verse 10 was a turning point, for he asked God to transform his heart and spirit so that he would always have the desire to obey God and walk in holiness. After we confess our sins and claim God's forgiveness, we must cooperate with the Holy Spirit and allow him to use God's Word to "heal" our hearts so that we won't stumble again. The Lord not only cleanses hearts, but he also creates new desires in our hearts so we want to obey him.

> If we confess our sins, He is faithful and just to forgive us our sins and to cleanse us from all unrighteousness.
>
> 1 John 1:9

32

> Restore to me *the joy of Your salvation*, and uphold me by Your generous Spirit.

PSALM 51:12

This psalm is one of David's prayers of confession as he sought God's forgiveness for his deliberate sins of adultery and murder (2 Sam. 11–12; Ps. 32). He did not lose his salvation, for salvation is as secure as God's covenant; but he lost the *joy* of his salvation. Happiness depends on happenings, what's going on *around* us; but joy depends on what's going on *within* us. Needless to say, David's inner man was a mess. Even the court singers didn't please him, for he prayed, "Make me hear joy and gladness" (Ps. 51:8). When we're out of fellowship with God, nothing goes right until we make things right with him and with anyone else involved.

Many people find themselves *enduring life*, and this is simply *desperation*. Henry David Thoreau wrote in the "Economy" chapter of *Walden*, "The mass of men lead lives of quiet desperation"—and this was before automobiles, airplanes, radios, Hollywood, television, and atomic power! Others are attempting to *escape life*, and their chief approach is *substitution*. They substitute prices for values, entertainment for enrichment, running here and there for sitting still at home with a quiet heart. They would rather be shouting in noisy crowds than at home enjoying family and friends. David already had several wives, so his affair with Bathsheba was pure selfishness. *Sin is often an expensive substitute for reality.*

God wants us neither to endure life nor try to escape life. He wants us to *enjoy* life and therefore he "gives us richly all things to enjoy" (1 Tim. 6:17). Life is filled with problems, battles, and burdens, but our response is neither desperation nor substitution but *transformation*. Jesus told his disciples that a woman experiences travail when she delivers a child, but after the child is born, she rejoices (John 16:20–22). *That's transformation.* The same baby that caused the pain also causes the joy! The defeats and disappointments of life can be transformed by the grace of God. "However, our God turned the curse into a blessing" (Neh. 13:2).

Sin is the enemy of joy, because sin is the devil's substitute for God's blessings. Yielding to temptation may seem easy and exciting at the time, but the consequences are difficult and expensive. David paid dearly for that meeting with Bathsheba, but after his repentance, he discovered what the Lord could do in turning curses into blessings. Remember how David numbered the people and was chastened by the Lord, who killed seventy thousand Israelites? (See meditation 15.) He ended up buying the property on which his altar had been built, and on that property Bathsheba's son Solomon built the temple! Only the Lord can take a man's two worst sins and make a temple out of them! This is not an excuse for deliberately committing sin, but it is an encouragement to repentant sinners. "I have trusted in Your mercy; my heart shall rejoice in Your salvation. I will sing to the LORD, because He has dealt bountifully with me" (Ps. 13:5–6).

If we lose the joy of our salvation, it isn't because the Lord has failed. Are we guilty of unconfessed sins? If not, perhaps the Lord is testing us or the devil is tempting us. How we feel is not the important thing. What's important is how we relate to God and his Word. Don't settle for enduring life or escaping life. God will help you enjoy life, not in spite of the problems but because of them. He turns curses into blessings!

Now may the God of hope fill you with all joy and peace in believing, that you may abound in hope by the power of the Holy Spirit.

Romans 15:13

33

Evening and morning and at noon I will pray, and
cry aloud, and *He shall hear my voice*.

PSALM 55:17

Your call is very important to us, so please hold." So
we hold and hold and hold as our call becomes more
and more important—but not important enough to
deserve a human response. Prayer isn't like that. God knows
what we need even before we call, but he wants us to call on
him *for our sake*, not for his. He longs to give us what we
need, but first we must ask. The phrase "He shall hear my
voice" actually involves three privileges.

As humans, created in the image of God, we have *the privilege of speech*. Many people take this privilege for granted
and abuse it, when speech is really a miracle that must be
guarded and used for God's glory. God has put something
in the human brain that enables us to learn to speak and to
mature our speech as we grow older. We learn to speak not
only among ourselves but also between ourselves and God.
Yes, we can pray silently and praise him silently, but it's better
to pray and praise audibly, even when we're alone. To help
a child learn the names of things and how to say them is a
frustrating delight, but we're participating in a miracle! Many
philosophers have concluded that, more than anything else,
speech is what distinguishes humans from animals.

As Christians, we have *the privilege of prayer*. Throughout the Bible, and especially in the book of Psalms, we find
God's people praying. In Psalm 65:2, God is addressed as
"You who hear prayer," which is a significant title. The prayer
"hear me" is found at least twenty-five times in the Psalms as
the saints address the Lord—and he *does* hear them! When
David wrote Psalm 55, he was in deep trouble and wanted

to fly away (vv. 4–8). He was in a storm (v. 8) and he was at war (vv. 18–21), and in spite of his military experience, he seemed to be unable to defeat the enemy. But God heard his cry and gave him the victory. Instead of flying off like a dove, he soared above like an eagle (Isa. 40:31) and was more than a conqueror (Rom. 8:37).

We who know Christ also have *the privilege of claiming God's promises.* The Bible contains many promises relating to prayer and many examples of people who prayed, and our Father in heaven is pleased when we trust him and act upon his Word. Daniel imitated David in praying three times a day (Dan. 6:10), and Paul tells us to "pray without ceasing" (1 Thess. 5:17). The Lord heard David's voice when he was in the cave (Ps. 57), and he heard the prayers of Hezekiah when the king was on his sickbed (Isa. 38). Peter was sinking into the Sea of Galilee when he cried, "Lord, save me" (Matt. 14:30), and the Lord heard him over the tumult of the storm and rescued him. When Peter was in prison in Jerusalem, the Lord heard the prayers of the believers in the house of Mary, mother of John Mark, and the Lord set Peter free (Acts 12). Paul and Silas were in prison in Philippi praising God and praying, and the Lord set them free (Acts 16:25–34). No matter where we are, the Lord will hear us if we are praying by faith and claiming his promises. Jonah was praying in the stomach of a great fish, and God heard him (Jonah 2); and God even hears the young ravens when they cry for food (Ps. 147:9).

Prayer changes things—and it also changes people, including those who find themselves in deep trouble and trust the Lord to deliver them. Is there anything too hard for the Lord?

> I love the LORD, because he has heard
> My voice and my supplications.
> Because He has inclined His ear to me,
> Therefore I will call upon Him as long as I live.
>
> Psalm 116:1–2

34

Awake, my glory! Awake, lute and harp! *I will awaken the dawn.*

PSALM 57:8

In chapter three of *Walden*, American naturalist Henry David Thoreau wrote that morning "was the most memorable season of the day . . . the awakening hour." Not everybody agrees with him. Thoreau may have been living in his cabin in the woods when he wrote those words; but when David wrote Psalm 57, he was living in a cave and hiding from King Saul, who wanted to kill him. "My soul is among lions. . . . They have prepared a net for my steps" (vv. 4, 6). Many people find morning the most difficult time of the day, but David began the day exalting the Lord (vv. 5, 11), praying about three awakenings that believers ought to experience daily.

"Lord, awaken my soul!" The word *glory* means "the inner person," so David was asking the Lord for a revival in his own soul. If his inner person wasn't receiving spiritual strength from the Lord, how could David overcome the enemy and serve the Lord? Without the help of the Lord, how could he lead his band of men and ultimately receive the throne? It has well been said that what life does to us depends on what life finds in us. David depended on the Lord, and the Lord never failed him. He wrote in Psalm 18, "It is God who arms me with strength, and makes my way perfect" (v. 32). Each morning, before we get our body moving, we must be sure the inner person is awake and alert. "I will sing of Your power; yes, I will sing aloud of Your mercy in the morning" (Ps. 59:16). One of the best ways to have your soul ready for the day is to go to sleep meditating on Scripture; then you will be ready for the morning devotional time. "But his delight

is in the law of the LORD, and in His law he meditates day and night" (Ps. 1:2).

"*Lord, awaken my song!*" David played beautifully on the lute and the harp and wrote many songs of praise and thanksgiving. A new day means not only new blessings in our soul but also new praise on our lips that comes from our heart. David is praising the Lord *before the sun has come up*. Too often we find ourselves groaning in the morning instead of thanking the Lord and praising him for his mercies. "My voice you shall hear in the morning, O LORD; in the morning I will direct it to You, and I will look up" (Ps. 5:3). Anyone can sing after a victory, but it takes faith to sing before the battle, especially when you are outnumbered (2 Chron. 20:21–25).

"*Lord, awaken the sun!*" David hoped that his singing would wake up the sun, for he was among the many "early risers" in the Bible (1 Sam. 17:20). If we want God with us all the day, we should meet him at the beginning of the day, as did Abraham (Gen. 22:3), Jacob (Gen. 28:18), Moses (Exod. 8:20; 9:13; 24:4; 34:4), Joshua (Josh. 6:12; 7:16; 8:10), Job (Job 1:5), and Jesus (Mark 1:35–38; Luke 4:42; 21:35–38). Before we check the morning paper, before the phone starts ringing, before we get involved in our daily chores, we need to meet the Lord, meditate on the Word, pray, and wait on him to receive our directions for the day. The old hymn tells us to "take time to be holy," and the best time to take that time is at the beginning of the day. As busy as he was, Jesus was awake early in the morning, communing with his Father and then teaching in the temple.

No matter what may have happened the day before, each morning is a new beginning for us. The Lord will hear you, because he never sleeps (Ps. 121:3–4).

> His compassions fail not.
> They are new every morning;
> Great is Your faithfulness.
>
> Lamentations 3:22–23

35

My soul, *wait silently for God alone*, for my expectation is from Him.

I f we take these five words seriously, we will find ourselves overcoming three obstacles that get in the way of a successful Christian life: running ahead of God, giving orders to God, and interfering with God's plans.

Be patient and don't run ahead of God. "My soul, wait." We live in a society that is always in a hurry, and this includes Christians who seem to have lost the ability to wait on the Lord. In spite of our slogans and promotional schemes—"Reaching the world in our generation!"—the Lord is not in a hurry. He could have created the universe in an instant demonstration of power, but he chose to create it in six days. King Saul ran ahead of God and lost his crown, while Joseph in Egypt patiently waited in prison and one day received a crown. Jesus might have come to earth as an adult on Monday, died on the cross on Friday, and been resurrected on Sunday, but he stayed in Nazareth thirty years, spent three years ministering, and then died and rose again. Jesus is "Lord of the Sabbath" (Mark 2:28), which means he is Lord of our time. We must not be trapped by the competitive eagerness of the world. "Rest in the LORD, and wait patiently for Him" (Ps. 37:7) and be ready to act when he commands you.

Be silent and don't give orders to God. We not only live in a busy world, but we live in a noisy world. We have grown so used to the noise that we think it doesn't affect us, but it does. A doctor told me that the teens who drive amplifiers on wheels and listen to rock bands will probably have serious hearing loss by the time they enter their forties. I hope not. Jesus is not only the Lord of my time, but he is also the

76

Lord of my tongue. There is "a time to keep silence, and a time to speak" (Eccles. 3:7). The noisiest book in the Bible may be the book of Job, in which God, Satan, Job, Job's wife, and four of Job's friends argue about the character of God and the meaning of suffering. But the problems aren't solved until Job closes his mouth and lets God do the talking (Job 40:1–5; 42:1–6). The apostle Peter had advice for Jesus when he spoke of his death (Matt. 16:21–23) and also on the Mount of Transfiguration (17:1–7), but Jesus didn't follow it. It's easier to hear the Lord's Word and learn his plans when we aren't talking.

Be calm and don't interfere with God. To live the Christian life, we need "God alone." It's remarkable what God can do if we don't interfere with his plans but allow him to receive the glory. It's easy to be like Jacob and pray for help and then make our own plans (Gen. 32:6–21). Trusting is living without scheming, and we aren't smart enough to make better plans than God makes. In the original Hebrew text of Psalm 62, the word translated "only" or "alone" is used in verses 1, 2, 4, 5, 6, and 9. When Jesus announced his coming death, Peter interfered with his plans (Matt. 16:21–23), and in the garden, Peter drew his sword and tried to deliver Jesus (John 18:1–11). To interfere with God's plans is to rob ourselves of the best blessings he has planned for us.

This entire psalm tells us to focus entirely on the Lord, for he is our rock (vv. 2, 6, 7), our refuge (vv. 7–8), our salvation (vv. 1, 2, 6, 7), our defense (vv. 2, 6), and our glory (v. 7). Jesus is the Lord of our time, so be patient and wait on him. He is the Lord of our speech, so be silent and don't advise him. He is the Lord of our plans, so let him have his way. The future is your friend when Jesus is your Lord.

36

> My soul, wait silently for God alone, for *my expectation is from Him.*

PSALM 62:5

Expectation means hope, and the major hope in the heart of the Christian should be the return of Jesus Christ for his church. Paul calls it "the blessed hope" (Titus 2:13). "Hope in itself is a species of happiness," wrote Samuel Johnson, "and perhaps the chief happiness which the world affords." His contemporary Alexander Pope wasn't that optimistic when he wrote, "Hope springs eternal in the human breast: / Man never is, but always to be blest." People fix their hopes on different things—the banker, the physician, the new employer—but the dedicated Christian fixes his hope wholly on God. "And now, Lord, what do I wait for? My hope is in You" (Ps. 39:7). Our hope in Christ is not the "hope so" of wishful thinking, because it is certain and brings many blessings to each of us.

Purity. "And everyone who has this hope in Him purifies himself, just as He is pure" (1 John 3:3). This was also Paul's prayer for the Thessalonian Christians (1 Thess. 5:22–23) and it should be our prayer. Just as an engaged couple keeps pure as they eagerly anticipate their wedding, so does the church, the bride of Christ (Rev. 19:7–9).

Faithful service. "Blessed are those servants whom the master, when he comes, will find watching. . . . Therefore you also be ready, for the Son of Man is coming at an hour you do not expect" (Luke 12:37, 40). To quote Samuel Johnson again, "Where there is no hope, there can be no endeavor." The farmer works hard to prepare the soil, plant the seed, and cultivate the plants, because he wants to reap a harvest. Students apply themselves because they want to graduate and go on with life. Jesus said, "And behold, I am coming quickly, and My reward is with Me, to give to every one according to his work" (Rev. 22:12).

Comfort. The return of Christ not only means rewards for the faithful but also reunion for the sorrowful (1 Thess. 4:13–18).We shall again be with our Christian loved ones and friends who have died, and we shall always be with the Lord and with them.

Joy. Paul writes that "rejoicing in hope" is normal Christian behavior (Rom. 12:12). No matter what circumstances we may be in, knowing that the best is yet to come ought to put joy in our hearts. G. K. Chesterton wrote, "Hope is the power of being cheerful in circumstances which we know to be desperate." Happiness depends on happenings, but true joy depends on our relationship with the Lord. "Rejoice in the Lord always. . . . The Lord is at hand" (Phil. 4:4–5).

Stability. "This hope we have as an anchor of the soul, both sure and steadfast, and which enters the Presence behind the veil" (Heb. 6:19). Material anchors go down to the depths, but our spiritual anchor goes heavenward where Jesus now is and keeps us from drifting away from our Christian profession (Heb. 2:1). Material anchors hold the ship still, but our anchor enables us to move ahead in the Christian life (Heb. 6:1) and not to "sink" in life's storms.

As we wait before the Lord and meditate and pray, the Spirit and the Word increase our hope. Take time to read Romans 15:4, 13—and rejoice in hope!

> The hope of the righteous will be gladness,
> But the expectation of the wicked will perish.
>
> Proverbs 10:28

37

> Do not cast me off in *the time of old age*; do not forsake me when my strength fails.
>
> PSALM 71:9

American poet Ogden Nash said that old age arrives when our descendants outnumber our friends, and for some people, that may be true. One thing is sure: old age does come, but with the help of the Lord we can deal with it like Christians. What does this mean?

We avoid foolishness. "There are old fools as well as young fools," a friend said to me as we discussed a church problem. Paul admonished the older men and women in the church family to be worthy of respect and honor God, among other things (Titus 2:2). Throughout Scripture, the emphasis is on the wisdom of the elderly. "Wisdom is with aged men, and with length of days, understanding" (Job 12:12). King Rehoboam made the mistake of following the counsel of his young friends, and the nation divided into Israel and Judah, but his father Solomon wrote about "an old and foolish king" who wouldn't listen to reason (Eccles. 4:13).

We oppose fretfulness. In Ecclesiastes 12:1–7, Solomon graphically describes some of the problems of old age that make us fret. The body doesn't function as it once did, we are alarmed by even the least sounds, and we are afraid of heights and fast travel. Things we once enjoyed no longer appeal to us and we have a tendency to fret and criticize. These reactions are probably symptoms of our resistance to change and our fear of being left behind. It doesn't help the ego when your youngest grandchild knows more about computers than you do! But God will not cast us off in old age (Ps. 71:9, 18) and has even promised to carry us (Isa. 46:4). As the Lord enables us, we should quit complaining and do what we can to help and encourage others.

We major on faithfulness. The familiar Christmas story recorded in Luke 1–2 introduces us to four godly elderly people: Zacharias and Elizabeth, the parents of John the Baptist, and Simeon and Anna, worshipers in the temple. Because they were faithful to the Lord, others heard about the Savior God had sent into the world. "The silver-haired head is a crown of glory, if it be found in the way of righteousness" (Prov. 16:31). "Senior saints" should be such an example of godliness that the younger people can joyfully obey Leviticus 19:32, "Stand up in the presence of the aged, show respect for the elderly and revere your God: I am the LORD" (TNIV). But the elderly should also do their part by teaching and encouraging those who are younger (2 Tim. 2:2).

We manifest fruitfulness. "The righteous shall flourish like a palm tree, he shall grow like a cedar in Lebanon. . . . They shall still bear fruit in old age; they shall be fresh and flourishing" (Ps. 92:12, 14). During my years of ministry, some of the greatest Christians I have met were men and women who could have retired but determined instead to "serve him to the end." The well-known British preacher and author F. B. Meyer told a friend, "I do hope my Father will let the river of my life go flowing fully to the finish. I don't want it to end in a swamp." That has also been my prayer. I want to be fresh, fruitful, and flourishing! Now in my eighties, I can't do all the things I used to do, but by God's grace I want to keep doing the things he lets me do.

The time of old age reveals what is truly important to us and it gives us one more opportunity to serve the Lord and help to reach those who have never trusted him. We can walk with the Lord and allow the rivers of water to flow and bless others (John 7:37–39), or we can live selfishly and stop bearing fruit for his glory. Let's make the right decision!

> They will still bear fruit in old age,
> they will stay fresh and green.
>
> Psalm 92:14 TNIV

38

I went into the sanctuary of God; Then I understood their end.

PSALM 73:17

This psalm was written by the Levite Asaph, one of the worship leaders in the Jewish sanctuary (1 Chron. 16:1–6, 37). He also wrote Psalms 50 and 74–83. In Psalm 73, he tells how he temporarily lost his song and how, with God's help, he got it back again. He was discouraged because the worldly crowd seemed to be prospering while the godly believers were suffering, and it didn't seem right. But when he went into the sanctuary, the dwelling place of God, he became a changed man. From his experience, we learn three basic instructions for life.

Don't look around and become a "people watcher." Asaph wasn't the first person to get discouraged because the wicked seem to prosper while the godly are suffering. Job was bothered by this problem (Job 21) and so were Jeremiah (Jer. 12), David (Ps. 37), and Habakkuk (Hab. 1). But focusing on what unbelievers *do* and *have* means walking by sight and not by faith. Asaph learned that the worldly life is only a dream and a mirage (Ps. 73:20), while believers are in touch with reality and eternity. We should not be envious of the lost because their destiny is to perish (vv. 17, 27); neither should we be envious of other Christians, because we don't have either the ability or the authority to pass judgment on other believers (Rom. 14:4). When you are in the sanctuary, in fellowship with God, you shouldn't look at other people or even at yourself. Your focus should be on the Lord.

Do look back and recall God's goodness (Ps. 73:1). "Oh, taste and see that the LORD is good" (34:8). If we forget the goodness of God, there may be something wrong with our spiritual "taste buds" because we are feeding on the wrong kind of food. Our Lord is present with us and holds us and guides us (73:23–24). We have the Holy Spirit within to teach us and empower us, and we have the Word of God and its multitude of promises to encourage us. And don't forget that some of the pain we endure in this world is the result of our being Christians and being light and salt. "Yes, all who desire to live godly in Christ Jesus will suffer persecution" (2 Tim. 3:12). We are prone to take God's blessings for granted and to complain about the trials that God permits so we can grow in grace. "God is the strength of my heart," Asaph said, "and my portion forever" (Ps. 73:26). In the midst of poverty, sorrow, and pain, Job said to his wife, "Shall we indeed accept good from God, and shall we not accept adversity?" (Job 2:10). In fact, on the basis of Romans 8:28, the experiences we have filed under "bad" will one day be classified as "good." When we "count our blessings," we drive envy out of our hearts and bring the praises of God to our lips.

Do look ahead and rejoice over future glory. "You will guide me with Your counsel, and afterward receive me to glory" (Ps. 73:24). Jesus endured the cross because of "the joy set before him" (Heb. 12:2 TNIV), which includes the joy of presenting the Church, his Bride, to the Father in heaven (Jude 24). Memories too often bring defeat, but anticipating fulfilled promises will bring joy and victory as we are "looking unto Jesus, the author and finisher of our faith" (Heb. 12:2). When the burdens are heavy and the battles fierce, and you start to envy others, meditate on the words of Jesus in John 13:7, "What I am doing you do not understand now, but you will know after this." Faith in his Word moves you into the sanctuary of his presence and provides all you need to win the battle.

> And we know that all things work together for good to those who love God, to those who are the called according to His purpose.
>
> Romans 8:28

39

How often they provoked Him in the wilderness,
and grieved Him in the desert.

PSALM 78:40

It has often been said that God took Israel out of Egypt in one night, but that it took him forty years to get Egypt out of Israel. Liberty is no guarantee of maturity. After being in bondage for centuries, the Jewish people had to overcome their slave mentality or they would never have been able to conquer their enemies and claim their inheritance. Israel's complaining and criticizing was a constant irritation to both Moses and the Lord. But this juvenile attitude is also true of many of God's people today who should be enjoying their freedom in Christ. If you find yourself thinking or saying any of the following statements, you are still living like a slave and you need to start moving toward maturity.

"Life is such a burden!" Life was a burden to the Jews in Egypt, and they had to obey orders or be punished. Children obey because they fear punishment, but mature people obey out of love and devotion. God led Israel to Sinai, where he displayed his glory and gave them the laws that would protect them and guide them. The people were to love the Lord their God and obey him in every area of life, but this was not slavery. It is the highest kind of freedom when love binds God's people to the Lord and one another. If life is a burden to you, read and obey Matthew 11:28–30.

"I must have security!" Yes, there were dangers in the desert, but the Lord was with his people to protect them and provide for them. "The LORD is my shepherd; I shall not want" (Ps. 23:1). The Lord made sure their shoes and clothes didn't wear out and that they had their daily bread, and he fought against their enemies and gave Israel victory. Loving

and doing the will of God is the surest source of security. The safest place in the world is in the will of God.

"I don't see why that happened!" Mature believers walk by faith and not by sight (2 Cor. 5:7). The Lord was preparing his people for the battles and blessings that they would meet in the Promised Land. Every temptation we overcome can help to sharpen our spiritual eyes and strengthen our spiritual muscles, and every trial can help us grow in grace.

"Lord, I've had enough trouble!" During their wilderness journey, the Jews experienced hunger, thirst, and the attacks of enemy armies, and their usual response was to complain. None of us is entitled to anything. All we receive is by the grace of God and we should not complain.

"I'm entitled to get what I want!" The people asked for meat to eat and God gave it to them, but many of them died because of this (Num. 11). Have you grown enough in your spiritual life that you can be thankful for unanswered prayer?

"Oh for the good old days!" Whenever the going got tough, the Jews wanted to go back to Egypt, back to slavery and pain. But that was not God's plan. "Let us go on to perfection [maturity]" is our challenge (Heb. 6:1). Growing from babyhood to adulthood isn't easy, but who wants to remain in the cradle and the playpen?

Provoking God by our childishness and rebellion only grieves him and robs us of the best he has planned for us. We who belong to Christ are no longer "of the world" (John 17:16), but is there anything of the world still in our hearts? If so, then let's confess it and forsake it so that, like Israel of old, we don't compromise and get back into bondage. Our citizenship is in heaven (Phil. 3:20).

> Behold, to obey is better than sacrifice,
> And to heed than the fat of rams.
>
> 1 Samuel 15:22

40

> You have a mighty arm; strong is Your hand, and high is Your right hand.

There are so many power tools and electronic instruments today that the strength of a worker's arms doesn't matter. But it was not so in Bible times, when both workers and warriors needed strong muscles. God doesn't depend on the strength of *our* arms; we are the ones who depend on the strength of *his* arms—and they are strong and mighty. Once we think we are strong, we will soon find ourselves weak. King Uzziah "was marvelously helped till he became strong" (2 Chron. 26:15). Paul had it right when he wrote, "For when I am weak, then I am strong" (2 Cor. 12:10). When we put our trust in God, it is his mighty arm that enables us to do his will.

The arm of God the Creator. "Ah, Lord God! Behold, You have made the heavens and the earth by Your great power and outstretched arm. There is nothing too hard for You" (Jer. 32:17). The creation beneath us, around us, above us, and within us convinces us day and night of the incredible power and wisdom of God. What men call "scientific law" is just their way of explaining the wonderful principles God has built into his universe. They remind us that nothing is too hard for the Lord. In his Sermon on the Mount, Jesus pointed to the weak flowers and birds and reminded us that if God cares for them, surely he will care for us. Therefore, don't worry!

The arm of God the Deliverer. The power of God's arm is also seen in human history. After crossing the Red Sea on dry ground, Israel sang and announced that fear and dread would fall upon their enemies by the greatness of God's arm (Exod.

15:16). When they were about to enter the Promised Land, Moses assured them of God's help: "The LORD brought us out of Egypt with a mighty hand and an outstretched arm" (Deut. 26:8). The Father has "delivered us from the power of darkness and conveyed us into the kingdom of the Son of His love" (Col. 1:13).

The arm of God the Conqueror. God brought Israel out of Egypt so that he might bring them into their inheritance, and he helped them to conquer their enemies. "For they did not gain possession of the land by their own sword, nor did their own arm save them; but it was Your right hand, Your arm . . . because You favored them" (Ps. 44:3). We possess our spiritual inheritance in Christ by trusting God and the power of his arm (Eph. 1:19; Col. 1:29).

The arm of God the Savior. "Who has believed our report? And to whom has the arm of the LORD been revealed?" (Isa. 53:1). Our salvation wasn't achieved by sacrificing animals or by doing good works. It was the death of Jesus Christ on the cross and his resurrection that purchased our salvation. God bared his strong arm at Calvary and the empty tomb, and conquered sin and death.

The arm of God the Caregiver. "He will gather his lambs with His arm, and carry them in His bosom" (Isa. 40:11). Jesus the loving Shepherd searches for the lost lamb, finds it, carries it over his shoulders—note the plural—and brings it home (Luke 15:5). The lamb is safe in the shepherd's arms and with the flock in the fold.

God has mighty arms and they never weaken or fail!

The eternal God is your refuge, and underneath are the everlasting arms.

Deuteronomy 33:27

41

> Remember *how short my time is*; for what futility
> have You created all the children of men?
>
> PSALM 89:47

Someone has said that time is a great healer but a poor beautician, and as I grow older, I agree. Everybody alive gets older, but not everybody reveals or repairs in the same way the damage that aging brings. There are occasions when time seems to move at the speed of light, and there are occasions when time seems to creep like late afternoon traffic. One thing is sure: time is always on the move and each of us must decide how we will handle it.

We can waste our time in futility. Thirty-eight times in the book of Ecclesiastes we find the word *vanity* or *meaninglessness*. One of my professors told us the Hebrew word translated *vanity* means "what is left after the soap bubble breaks." King Solomon carefully examined many aspects of human life before he wrote Ecclesiastes, and he came to the conclusion that life is meaningless. Life without meaning is merely existence, not real life. We can work hard and perhaps replace the money we have spent, but we can't get back the time we have wasted. If the Lord asked the people on this "vanity track" why he should allow them to live, they would have no answer. Living for the vanities of this world is a waste of life.

We can spend our time in mere activity. God "gives us richly all things to enjoy" (1 Tim. 6:17), but not all enjoyment brings enrichment to our lives. God gives to us *richly* because he wants us to be enriched. As we mature in the Lord, we want experiences that will glorify God and build us up spiritually. Real life means giving as well as receiving. Jesus said, "Most assuredly, I say to you, unless a grain of wheat falls into the ground and dies, it remains alone; but if it dies, it produces much grain" (John 12:24). If you live your life only for yourself, you will lose it, but if you give your life to Christ, you will save it and help to save others. Activity alone is busyness without blessing. We are living on substitutes.

We can invest our time in the eternal. Life involves stewardship. God gives us life at conception and eternal life at conversion, and with both experiences come gifts and abilities to be used for God's glory. God didn't make me an athlete or a mechanic, but he did give me a love for words—reading them, studying them, learning from them, speaking and writing them. Since my teen years, the Bible has been my basic textbook and I thank God for all he has taught me. This doesn't mean that every believer must become a preacher or teacher, but that each of us must develop our gifts and use them to serve others and to glorify the Lord in whatever calling God gives us. We must live "with eternity's values in view." "The world is passing away," says 1 John 2:17, "and the lust of it; but he who does the will of God abides forever." We are not wasting time or spending time; we are investing our time in that which will last forever.

Contrasted to eternity, life is brief and time goes past swiftly. Do we realize this? It seems but yesterday that I was married and two years later became a father. Now my wife and I have great-grandchildren! Where has the time gone? It's gone into eternity and one day we shall follow it. We shall stand at the judgment seat of Christ and our works will be judged.

Let's invest our short lives in that which is eternal. The dividends are immeasurable, now and forever.

Moreover it is required in stewards that one be found faithful.

1 Corinthians 4:2

42

Your testimonies are very sure; holiness adorns
Your house, O LORD, forever.

right
PSALM 93:5

estimonies is one of the words for "Bible," the Word
of God. It comes from a Latin word that means "witness," which also gives us the English words *testify*
and *testament*. The Scriptures bear witness to the existence
of God and the character of God, his works and his will for
his people. What kind of a witness is the Bible?

The Bible is a royal testimony. "The LORD reigns" from
an eternal throne (Ps. 93:1–2) and always will. "The LORD is
King forever and ever" (Ps. 10:16; *see* 1 Tim. 1:17). In ancient
times, when the king spoke, the people listened and obeyed.
"Where the word of a king is, there is power, and who may
say to him, 'What are you doing?'" (Eccles. 8:4). We must
never take the Bible for granted, for the King of the universe
deigns to speak to us! When we open our hearts and open
the Bible, God opens his mouth; and if he doesn't speak to
us, we had better quickly find out why. Is there sin in our life?
Are we in too big of a hurry in our reading?

The Bible is a contemporary testimony. The psalmist uses
the verb *are*. This is present tense, because what God said
centuries ago still speaks to us today. God's Word does not
change, but languages do change; and for this reason Bible
scholars must revise the text from time to time. As we read
Scripture, we "listen in" on what God says to the patriarchs,
the kings, the prophets, and the common people—but what
he says also speaks to us today. And we also hear what these
people said to God. God's Word is a *living book*, and its
message never grows old (Heb. 4:12; 1 Pet. 1:23). I smile when
people say, "Our pastor makes the Bible so relevant."

center
90

No matter how we mortals handle the Bible, *it is always relevant*. If we will but allow him, the Holy Spirit will prove it to us.

The Bible is a dependable testimony. "Your testimonies are very sure" (Ps. 93:5). God's throne is established (v. 2) and God's Word is established. Not every witness in court is dependable and some have been fined for contempt of court, but the witness of the Bible is always dependable. The people who say, "As sure as the world" ought to say, "As sure as the Word." Jesus said, "Heaven and earth will pass away, but My words will by no means pass away" (Matt. 24:35). Like storms on the ocean, the voices of the nations try to drown out the voice of the Lord, but his Word continues to speak (Ps. 93:3–4). God rebukes the defiant voices of the nations (Isa. 17:12–13) and even laughs at them (Ps. 2:1–4). Remember that when you read the newspaper or listen to the ten o'clock news.

The Bible is a transforming testimony. This short psalm ends on a personal note: if we love God's Word and seek to obey it, our lives will be transformed. "Holiness adorns Your house, O LORD, forever" (Ps. 93:5). The word *house* can refer either to the sanctuary of God or to the people of God. When the holy Bible is rightly understood and applied, it produces a holy people (2 Cor. 3:18). God rules his universe by *commandment* and not by committee or consensus. We never negotiate the will of God; we accept it and obey it.

> Why do the nations conspire
> and the peoples plot in vain?
>
> Psalm 2:1 TNIV

43

> *Exalt the LORD our God*, and worship at His footstool—He is holy.
>
> PSALM 99:5

It seems strange that the Holy Spirit should have to admonish us through the psalmist to worship the Lord and exalt him alone (Ps. 99:5, 9). Isn't exalting the Lord what you would expect from Christians? To exalt Christ ought to be the deepest desire of our hearts and the most natural expression of our lives. The word *exalt* comes from two Latin words: "out" (*ex*) and "high" (*altus*). To exalt the Lord means to lift him high, out from among the "celebrities" in this world. It means to magnify Christ in our witness, walk, work, and worship so that others can see how great he is. This psalm gives us three reasons why we should lovingly and faithfully magnify the Lord in today's godless society.

He reigns from a high and holy throne (vv. 1–3). Though we cannot see him, he is "high above all" and can never be dethroned. Our Savior Jesus Christ is enthroned with his Father in heaven (Heb. 1:3; 12:2), and together they are in complete control. The phrase "between the cherubim" (Ps. 99:1) takes us into the Holy of Holies of the sanctuary. The two gold cherubim were a part of the mercy seat that sat on the top of the ark of the covenant. This was the throne of God in the nation of Israel. The glory of God dwelt in the Holy of Holies, because the throne of God and the glory of God go together. But this glorious throne is also a throne of grace where our Savior ministers to us and hears our prayers (Heb. 4:14–16), for grace and glory go together (Ps. 84:11). This is why "hallowed be Your name" is the first request in the Lord's Prayer (Matt. 6:9). If our requests don't glorify him, why should we ask for them? Let's exalt the perfect King!

He serves as a high and holy Judge (Ps. 99:4–5). How much justice, righteousness, and equity do we see in our world today? The staggering backup of cases in our court system discourages some people from even attempting to get justice. The Lord is wise and mighty and able to see the human heart and give accurate judgment with wisdom. "The LORD executes righteousness and justice for all who are oppressed" (Ps. 103:6), if not in this life then certainly in the next. When the books are opened, the Lord will see to it that the righteous will be vindicated and rewarded and the wicked condemned and punished. "He is the Rock, His work is perfect; for all His ways are justice, a God of truth and without injustice; righteous and upright is He" (Deut. 32:4). God has "appointed a day on which He will judge the world in righteousness by the Man whom He has ordained" (Acts 17:31). Let's exalt the perfect Judge!

He maintains a high and holy relationship (Ps. 99:6–9). My wife and I have visited London, England, many times, but we have never tried to walk past the guards at the gates of Buckingham Palace and force our way in to see the queen. But the children of God may come boldly to the throne of grace and fellowship with the Lord! The psalmist names Moses, Aaron, and Samuel, all of them great men, but we have more privileges in Christ than they did. Aaron could enter the Holy of Holies only once a year, yet we can live in the "secret place of the Most High" (Ps. 91:1). We can speak to God and he will speak to us from his Word. He is a God who forgives us when we confess our sins (1 John 1:9). As we worship him, the greatness of his attributes overwhelms us and transforms us. What privileges we have at the throne of grace!

> O LORD, You are my God.
> I will exalt You,
> I will praise Your name.
>
> Isaiah 25:1

44

Bless the LORD, O my soul, and *forget not all His benefits.*

PSALM 103:2

The word *benefit* comes from two Latin words that together mean "to do good." Because God *is* good, He *does* good. He cannot do evil. What he does may not seem good to us at the time, but if God does it, it is good—even Paul's thorn in the flesh (2 Cor. 12:7–10). "And we know that in all things God works for the good of those who love him, who have been called according to his purpose" (Rom. 8:28 TNIV). Three elements are involved in this matter of blessing the Lord for his benefits.

Memory—let's remember the Lord. In my pastoral ministry, I have visited people whose minds had moved into dementia, and the visit usually depressed me. When the memory stops functioning, people don't know themselves or others, nor do they know where they are or why they are there. Memory is a great gift from God and yet we take it for granted. Suppose each morning we had to relearn our name and address, the alphabet, the number system, plus the names of the people in our lives. We would almost be isolated from reality. The people of Israel frequently forgot God and worshiped the idols of the nations around them, and God had to discipline his people. In his farewell address to Israel, the book of Deuteronomy, Moses often said "remember" and "do not forget." Five times he said, "Remember that you were slaves in the land of Egypt." Whenever Israel forgot who they were and what God had done for them, they lapsed into sin and paid dearly for their disobedience. Every local church should have an annual "Heritage Sunday" and review the church's history to educate new members and remind everyone what God has done. To lose your history is to lose your identity.

Mercy—let's thank the Lord. God gave the Israelites the weekly Sabbath and seven annual "feasts" to remind them of his grace and mercy (Lev. 23). The nation also erected special memorials to bear witness of key historical events. Churches meet on the Lord's Day to commemorate Christ's resurrection, and they remember his death and forthcoming return when they meet at the Lord's Table. We also have special days such as Christmas, Good Friday, Easter Sunday, and Reformation Sunday, all of which memorialize special events in church history. Both the church at Ephesus and the church at Sardis needed their memories jogged (Rev. 2:5; 3:3), and perhaps some churches today have the same need.

Ministry—let's serve the Lord. Celebrating God's past work doesn't mean we ignore the present and future. But recalling past events can help us get fresh spiritual insight and motivation to serve the Lord today and plan for the future. A famous philosopher wrote, "He who does not know the past is condemned to repeat it." When Paul met with the Ephesian elders, he reviewed the past as a basis for assessing the present and planning for the future (Acts 20:17–38). If athletic teams can learn to be better players by reviewing replays of their games, can't we review the past and become better Christians?

Gratitude is a key element in the Christian life. Instead of imitating Israel and forgetting God's blessings and ignoring his counsel (Ps. 106:13), let's praise him and celebrate his goodness to us. God doesn't forget us, and there's no reason why we should forget him.

> I will not forget you.
> See, I have inscribed you on the palms of My hands.
>
> Isaiah 49:15–16

45

The LORD said to my Lord, "*Sit at My right hand*,
till I make Your enemies Your footstool."

PSALM 110:1

For at least two reasons, we must pay close attention to this psalm. First, it's about Jesus and his ministry to his church today; and second, the New Testament writers quote or refer to this psalm more than any other. It records what the Father said to the Son when Jesus returned to heaven, and it emphasizes several important truths about the Savior.

Jesus is a living Savior. He finished his redemptive work on earth (John 19:30), so he is not on the cross or in the tomb. He is alive! What a transformation the apostles experienced when this truth gripped them! We can live and serve Jesus today in "the power of His resurrection" (Phil. 3:10) because Christ lives in us by his Spirit (Gal. 2:20). The Spirit wants to empower us today so that we might bear witness to Jesus and his gospel. The world thinks Jesus is an ancient teacher who is now dead, but the Spirit wants to use us to demonstrate that he is alive and at work in this world. Are we available?

Jesus is an exalted Savior. During his days of ministry on earth, Jesus was an obedient, suffering servant, but God "has highly exalted Him" (Phil. 2:9) and "raised Him from the dead and seated Him at His right hand in the heavenly places, far above all" (Eph. 1:20–21). There is not now, nor has there been, nor will there ever be a person on earth whose name is higher than that of our Lord in heaven. Everything is "under His feet" (v. 22) and he is in complete control. Why should we be timid and afraid?

Jesus is a reigning Savior. Our Lord doesn't have to return to earth in order to be King, for he is King right now! "All authority has been given to Me in heaven and on earth," he told his disciples before he commissioned them and then ascended to heaven (Matt. 28:18–20). It is in that authority, and not our own ability, that we go forth to witness and to extend his kingdom. We can "reign in life" because he is reigning in heaven (Rom. 5:17). Furthermore, the Father has "raised us up together, and made us to sit together in the heavenly *places* in Christ Jesus" (Eph. 2:6). How much higher can we get and how much more authority can we receive?

Jesus is a ministering Savior. "We have such a High Priest, who is seated at the right hand of the throne of the Majesty in the heavens" (Heb. 8:1). The Epistle to the Hebrews explains our Lord's present ministry in heaven to enable his church to serve on earth. But don't get the false notion that the Father is angry at us, so Jesus has to intercede for us so we can receive the help we need. The Father and the Son work together to mature us and to enable us to glorify the Lord. Jesus is a great High Priest who knows our weaknesses and can give us the grace to help us in our times of need (4:14–16).

God has put all things under the feet of Jesus so that Jesus can put all our enemies under our feet and give us a life of joyful victory (2:5–9; Rom. 16:20). We don't fight *for* victory in our own strength but *from* victory, the victory Jesus has already won for us (Eph. 1:19–23). As we read the Word daily, meditate on it, yield ourselves to the Spirit, *and exercise faith*, we will receive from Jesus all we need to detect and defeat the enemy.

> You have made him to have dominion over the works
> of Your hands;
> You have put all things under his feet.
>
> Psalm 8:6

46

Let Your tender mercies come to me, that I may live; for *Your law is my delight.*

PSALM 119:77

Whatever delights us directs us, and whatever directs us determines our destiny; so we must be careful to cultivate a spiritual appetite. "Blessed are those who hunger and thirst for righteousness, for they shall be filled" (Matt. 5:6). When we delight in God's Word, we also delight in God's will. Jesus said, "My food is to do the will of Him who sent me, and to finish His work" (John 4:34). Either evil is sweet to our mouth (Job 20:12) or the Word of God is "sweeter than honey" in our mouth (Ps. 119:103). "Oh, taste and see that the LORD is good" (34:8).

God is sovereign and rules the universe. He has put definite laws into every kingdom—mineral, vegetable, animal, human, and the spiritual kingdom of God. If we defy these laws, the consequences are painful and might even be fatal. We learn the laws and principles of God's kingdom from the Word of God and as we obey what we learn. "But his delight is in the law of the LORD, and in His law he meditates day and night" (1:2).

I have the freedom to drive a car because I possess a license, but I obtained that license by studying a manual, being taught by a certified driver, and successfully passing a test. As long as I obey the traffic laws, I am free to drive. Scientists are able to study minerals, plants, animals, humans, and galaxies because the Creator has put into these kingdoms laws that do not change. NASA can send astronauts into space and bring them safely back to earth again because their technicians understand these laws and obey them.

Why don't more of God's people delight in reading and studying God's Word? The Holy Spirit who wrote the Bible lives in each believer and urges us to set aside time daily for Bible meditation and prayer, but some are too busy to "take time to be holy." Or perhaps no one has taught them the how and why of Bible meditation. It takes time for children to learn to feed themselves *and to enjoy the right foods*. If they eat too much "junk food" between meals, they will have no appetite for good nutrition.

If God's people will focus on what God's Word is, it will motivate them to make the Bible the most important book they possess. The Bible is everything we need for developing spiritual maturity. It is food for growing (Ps. 119:103; Matt. 4:4; 1 Pet. 2:2; Heb. 5:12–14), water for cleansing (Ps. 119:9; John 15:3; Eph. 5:26), a light to guide us (Ps. 119:105, 130), a sword to protect us (Eph. 6:17; Heb. 4:12), wealth to enrich us (Ps. 119:14, 72, 127, 162), and truth to transform us (John 17:17).

We always seem to find time to do the things that please us most, whether it be napping, shopping, fishing, or sending and receiving emails. Psalm 119:147–48 inform us that the psalmist arose not only early in the morning to meditate on the Word but also in the middle of the night. "I remember Your name in the night, O LORD, and I keep Your law" (v. 55). "At midnight I will rise to give thanks to You, because of Your righteous judgments" (v. 62).

Had Peter, James, and John not gone to sleep on the Mount of Transfiguration, they could have learned much as Jesus conversed with Moses and Elijah (Luke 9:32). Had Eutychus not fallen asleep, he would have benefited from Paul's address and not fallen out of the window (Acts 20:7–12). Let us wake up, and rise to study God's Word.

Now it is high time to awake out of sleep; for now our salvation is nearer than when we first believed.

Romans 13:11

47

I cry out to You; save me, and I will keep Your testimonies.

═══════════════════════ PSALM 119:146

The emphasis in Psalm 119 is on the Word of God and what it can do in our lives if we delight in it and do what it says. But there are other themes in this psalm that we must not ignore, and prayer is one of them. The psalmist cried out to God (vv. 145–47, 169) and there is evidence that the Lord answered him. We learn some basic prayer truths from his experience.

The godly have their enemies. Anyone who thinks that the Christian life is a peaceful voyage on a calm sea hasn't spent much time reading the New Testament. "Blessed are those who are persecuted for righteousness' sake," Jesus said, "for theirs is the kingdom of heaven" (Matt. 5:10); and Paul wrote, "Yes, and all who desire to live godly in Christ Jesus will suffer persecution" (2 Tim. 3:12). If unbelievers persecuted Jesus, they will certainly persecute those who follow Jesus and serve him (John 15:18–25). A man said to me, "I don't do any talking. I just live the life and that's my witness." But if your life is different from that of the world's crowd, they will notice it and ask you why, and that's your opportunity to witness. The psalmist was attacked by princes (Ps. 119:23) and lied about by the wicked (vv. 53, 61, 69). Evildoers oppressed him (vv. 115, 121, 122) and doubleminded lawbreakers despised him (vv. 113, 136, 141). Christians are the light of the world, but the world loves darkness rather than light because the light exposes their evil deeds (John 3:18–21).

The godly can pray for God's help. The psalmist called upon the Lord and cried out for the help he needed (vv. 145–47, 169). In Acts 4:23–31, the early church gives us a good example of

100

how we should pray when the world opposes us. The believers didn't ask God to remove the evil officials or shelter the church from persecution. They asked the Lord for boldness to continue their witness to the lost! The early church did not see persecution as a reason to quit but as an opportunity to bear witness to the leaders in Jerusalem. It's sad that church prayer meetings have been minimized in recent years. Perhaps we need some persecution.

The godly connect prayer with the Word of God. The believers praying in Acts 4 knew their Old Testament Scriptures, the only Bible they had. They quoted two verses of Psalm 2 from memory and applied them to the situation. When we are praying in the Spirit, he will remind us of verses we know and give us promises to claim. The church was following the example of the apostles who said "we will give ourselves continually to prayer and to the ministry of the word" (Acts 6:4). The Word and prayer must always go together. Prayer without the Word is heat without light, and the Word without prayer is light without heat! Jesus said that we need both. "If you abide in Me, and My words abide in you, you will ask what you desire, and it shall be done for you" (John 15:7). Samuel, the godly Old Testament leader, taught the same truth. "Moreover, as for me, far be it from me that I should sin against the Lord in ceasing to pray for you; but I will teach you the good and the right way" (1 Sam. 12:23). Prayer and the Word!

> Let my cry come before you, O Lord;
> Give me understanding according to Your word.
>
> Psalm 119:169

48

My lips shall utter praise, for You teach me Your statutes.

Here is a believer with *a balanced life*. We don't know who wrote Psalm 119, but we do know the concerns of his heart: learning the Word of God, praying for himself and others, and praising the Lord for answered prayer. The psalmist didn't have an easy life, but he did have a balanced life as he spent time in the Word, prayed, and gave thanks to God. A friend of mine used to say, "Blessed are the balanced, for they won't fall on their faces." If each day we will set aside time for the Word, prayer, and praise, God will do the rest. It's good to be devoted Bible students and grow in the knowledge of the Lord, but we must be careful not to stuff our heads and starve our hearts. "Knowledge puffs up, but love edifies" (1 Cor. 8:1). Along with studying we need praying, the kind of praying that will make it easier for the Holy Spirit to transform us through the Word (2 Cor. 3:18). But worship is also essential, for when we worship God, we get our eyes off ourselves and our needs and lose ourselves in the grace and glory of the Lord. Both private and corporate worship help focus our hearts and minds on the Lord, and this encourages and enables us in our walk and our work.

Here is a believer with *a disciplined life*. If disciples are not disciplined, there is something wrong with their discipleship. The psalmist arose before dawn to spend time with the Lord (Ps. 119:147), and he also communed with God during the night seasons (v. 148). "At midnight I will rise and give thanks to You" (v. 62). Paul and Silas turned the midnight hour into a miracle hour as they prayed to God and praised him in the Philippian prison, and many people were saved

(Acts 16:25–34). But the psalmist also wrote, "Oh, how I love Your law! It is my meditation all the day" (Ps. 119:97). This doesn't suggest that believers neglect their work and never read anything but the Bible. Evangelist D. L. Moody used to warn believers against "being so heavenly minded they were no earthly good." We live in a real world with real people and we dare not ignore our human responsibilities. Our devotion to the Lord ought to make us better citizens, family members, neighbors, and workers.

Here is a believer with *a surrendered life*. His heart, mind, and will (vv. 7–8) and his lips and tongue (vv. 171–72) belonged to the Lord, and so did his time. "Seven times a day I praise You" (v. 164). Do that long enough and praising God will be a blessed "holy habit" that will help transform your life. He asked God to give him "good judgment and knowledge" (v. 66) as well as a knowledge of the Word. A surrendered life has priorities; we don't merely choose between good and bad but also between better and best. We "seek first the kingdom of God and His righteousness" (Matt. 6:33) and give Jesus the place of preeminence (Col. 1:18). We should say with David, "I trust in You, O LORD . . . my times are in Your hand" (Ps. 31:14–15).

Here is a believer with a life *motivated by love*. If we want our lips to utter God's praise, then our hearts must be filled with love for God, God's Word, God's people, and God's service (119:47–48, 97, 132, 140, 165). Devotion in the heart helps to give direction to the mind and discipline to the will.

For Christ's love compels us.
2 Corinthians 5:14 TNIV

49

There is forgiveness with You, that You may be feared.

PSALM 130:4

Believers who honestly examine their own hearts know when they need forgiveness from the Lord. The Holy Spirit has a loving way of convicting us. Those who don't examine their hearts just keep pretending they are righteous and refuse to face facts. "If we say that we have no sin, we deceive ourselves, and the truth is not in us" (1 John 1:8).

When we know we have sinned, we know that only the Lord can forgive us. Judas confessed his sins to the religious leaders, but they couldn't help him. Overwhelmed by his burden, he went out and hanged himself. Peter had also sinned, but he wept bitter tears of repentance and settled the matter with Jesus privately (Luke 24:34; 1 Cor. 15:5).

"Man, your sins are forgiven you," Jesus said to the paralytic who was lowered from the roof into the house where he was teaching (Luke 5:20). This statement upset the religious leaders present and they accused him of blasphemy, but Jesus is God and there is forgiveness of sins with him. He said to a weeping ex-prostitute, "Your sins are forgiven. . . . Your faith has saved you. Go in peace" (7:48, 50). These words also offended the religious leaders, but they gave new life and a new beginning to the woman.

Because Jesus is the Son of God and the Savior of the world, he has the authority to forgive sins. His sacrificial death on the cross and his triumphant resurrection make it possible for sinners to be forgiven and born into the family of God. "In Him we have redemption from our sins, the forgiveness of sins, according to the riches of His grace" (Eph. 1:7). This miracle is not the result of our good works, because salvation is wholly the gift of God. Grace is love that pays a price to save people who don't deserve it. God in his grace gives us what we don't deserve, and in his mercy he doesn't give us what we do deserve. Jesus didn't deserve punishment; *we deserved it.*

During the Old Testament days, on each Day of Atonement (Lev. 16) two goats stood before the sanctuary. The high priest killed one of them and took some of its blood behind the veil into the Holy of Holies and sprinkled it on the golden mercy seat that covered the ark. Then he went outside, put his hands on the head of the living goat, and confessed the sins of the nation. A man then led the living goat out into the wilderness, never to be seen again. We have here two pictures of forgiveness: the blood covering the people's sins and the sins taken away, never to be seen again. "As far as the east is from the west, so far has He removed our transgressions from us" (Ps. 103:12).

Then what? The people certainly should have rejoiced to know that they were forgiven. "Blessed are those whose transgressions are forgiven, whose sins are covered" (Ps. 32:1 TNIV). The blood of animals covered their sins, but "the blood of Jesus Christ His Son cleanses us from all sin" (1 John 1:7). This should draw us so close to the Lord that we will love God more and dedicate ourselves anew to do his will. "Serve the LORD with fear, and rejoice with trembling" (Ps. 2:11). We are not forgiven that we may repeat our sins, but we must "go and sin no more" (John 8:11). The balance of godly fear and godly joy is not easy to maintain, but it's one of the essentials for godly living.

Shall we continue in sin that grace may abound? Certainly not!

Romans 6:1–2

50

LORD, *my heart is not haughty*, nor my eyes lofty.
Neither do I concern myself with great matters,
nor with things too profound for me.

PSALM 131:1

We cannot stand still in the Christian life, for if we do, we will soon start going backward and losing ground. The best way to avoid this peril is for us to be constantly moving ahead towards spiritual maturity (Heb. 6:1). God wants us to "grow in the grace and knowledge of our Lord and Savior Jesus Christ" (2 Pet. 3:18). If we have healthy habits, physical maturity is automatic. Social maturity is learned gradually, but spiritual maturity demands discipline, devotion, sacrifice, and service. Consider the possibilities.

We can remain spiritual babies. Weaning is usually a crisis experience for children because they think they have been rejected by a mother who no longer loves them. What they don't realize is that weaning is proof that their mother *does* love them and wants to lead them to the freedom of growing up. Children find dependence on their mother to be a safe and comfortable situation and they don't want to lose it, but losing it is essential to finding the freedom and opportunities of adulthood. This demands humility, submission, and obedience on the part of the child; otherwise, the mother will find herself with a pampered, selfish, disobedient, and demanding child. So it is in the spiritual life: the Lord lovingly weans us away from the temporary childish things that fascinate us (1 Cor. 13:11) and moves us from milk to solid food (Heb. 5:12–14).

We can pretend to be mature. This means "keeping up appearances" and concerning ourselves with adult matters about which we know nothing. We carry a large study Bible to church, but we haven't opened it all week. We go from conference to conference and take notes that we file away in a drawer and never apply to our life. We accept service opportunities that are beyond us, but we make no lasting contribution to the work at all. Like the church at Sardis, we have a name that we are alive, but we are really dead (Rev. 3:1–6). G. Campbell Morgan called this "reputation without reality" and Jesus called it hypocrisy. But masquerades eventually end and the masks come off, and then we discover that we've been childish but not childlike and our so-called humility reeks with pride. Children who pretend to be adults are grotesque, not cute, and nobody takes them seriously.

We can pay the price and start maturing. Spiritual maturity is not a destination, it's a journey; and the journey doesn't end until we see Jesus—then a new journey begins. Mature people know themselves, accept themselves, improve themselves, and give themselves to the Lord to serve others. They know what they can do and where they "fit in," and they don't campaign for authority and visibility. They just trust God to help them do their work well to the glory of Jesus. More ministries are harmed by pride than by any other sin. Pride robs us, but humility makes us receptive and rewards us with spiritual growth we may not always detect ourselves.

I read about a committee member who opposed almost every step toward progress by saying, "If you do that it will make me stumble and the Bible is against that." Finally the pastor replied, "I suggest you grow up and learn how to walk so you don't stumble so much." A haughty heart and a pair of lofty eyes can do a lot of damage.

God resists the proud, but gives grace to the humble.

1 Peter 5:5

51

He sends out His command to the earth; *His word runs very swiftly.*

I t's becoming more and more difficult to receive and digest the news, whether it's about politics, sports, the economy, or just local happenings. Why? Because there's so much of it (they call it "information overload") and much of it is very discouraging. But Christians can face facts with courage and maintain a quiet spirit *because God is at work in the world right now.* His Word is living and powerful (Heb. 4:12) and always accomplishes his purposes (Isa. 55:10–11). God's servants may be imprisoned, but God's Word cannot be imprisoned (2 Tim. 2:9). Psalm 147 informs us that God is at work today in nature (vv. 8–9, 15–18) and in the affairs of cities and nations (vv. 2–5, 12–14, 19–20), especially Israel. To accomplish his plans for Israel, God worked through pagan rulers like Nebuchadnezzar, Darius, and even Caesar.

Not only is God's living Word now at work in this world, but *God is using his people to spread that Word.* Paul commended the believers in Thessalonica because, like trumpeters, they "sounded" the gospel for miles around (1 Thess. 1:8–9). This reminds me of the royal messengers the Persian king sent out to tell his Jewish subjects the good news of their deliverance. "The couriers who rode on royal horses went out, hastened and pressed on by the king's command" (Esther 8:14). Our King has commanded us to take the gospel to every nation, and we have better ways of doing it than did the messengers in Esther's day. Why should we delay? More than one pioneer missionary has been asked, "How long have your people known this gospel? Why didn't you come sooner?" Are we a part of God's worldwide team for spreading the gospel message?

God's people support these messengers through prayer. "Finally, brethren, pray for us, that the word of the Lord may run swiftly and be glorified" (2 Thess. 3:1). The Word is on the move but we must back it up with prayer (Acts 6:4). If we pray in faith, God can remove the obstacles and provide the opportunities that his workers need (1 Cor. 16:9). God may not work as quickly as we desire and we may find ourselves asking "How long, O Lord? How long?" But God promises that "in due season we shall reap if we do not lose heart" (Gal. 6:9). I believe that earnest prayer is the greatest need in our churches today. In spite of his great gifts and education, Paul repeatedly asked the churches to pray for him, because gifts and training without prayer have no power to accomplish God's will. Paul prayed for the churches and for individuals in the churches. Are we following his example?

God's Word is running swiftly throughout the world, even though we can't see all that the Lord is accomplishing; but one day in heaven we will see how the Lord used our financial investments and prayers to expedite his work. Our text says that God "sends out His command to the earth." God "now commands all men everywhere to repent" (Acts 17:30). The gospel is not simply a message; it's a command from the King! Commercial enterprises get their message and their products into almost every corner of our world. Why can't we do the same with the good news of the gospel?

Behold, I bring you good tidings of great joy which will be to all people.

Luke 2:10

52

Incline your ear to wisdom, and apply your heart to understanding.

PROVERBS 2:2

W isdom is the major theme of the book of Proverbs. It means the skillful use of knowledge and experience as we obey the Lord, so that he can build our character and give us success. Success doesn't always mean material wealth, but it does mean the enrichment of our life so that we can enrich others. For us to have these blessings, five factors are involved.

Intention. Some people read the Bible daily just out of habit or to quiet their conscience, but neither approach is adequate. Our intention must be to please the Lord, to learn more about him, and to grow in grace so we can serve him better. We want to build an enriching relationship with the Lord through his words, "for they are life to those who find them and health to all their flesh" (Prov. 4:22). The Bible should be read like a love letter, not like a manual on how to file your income tax or repair your lawnmower. "As newborn babes, desire the pure milk of the word, that you may grow thereby" (1 Pet. 2:2).

Attention. "Hear, my children, the instruction of a father, and give attention to know understanding" (Prov. 4:1). Whether we read the Bible standing, sitting, or lying in bed, our heart, mind, and will must be standing at attention, ready to learn and obey. "Therefore take heed how you hear," Jesus said (Luke 8:18). Whether we are alone reading the Bible or in a congregation hearing the Bible read, we must pay attention; it is the voice of the Lord speaking. Our inner eyes and ears must be open (Eph. 1:17–18; 2 Tim. 4:4) to see and hear truth. To read or hear in a routine manner is to miss the message God has for us. The enemy will do all he can to distract us, but we must resist him and keep our attention fixed on God and his Word.

Meditation. Meditation is to the inner person what digestion is to the outer person: it makes the truth a part of our very being. We must welcome the Scriptures joyfully as a gift from God and not treat the Bible like any other book (1 Thess. 2:13). Other books can instruct the mind, but the Bible also nurtures and strengthens the heart (Matt. 4:4; Jer. 15:16). To meditate means to think over the passage, to relate it to other passages, and to apply it to our own lives. I enjoy tracing the cross-references and seeing how Scripture explains Scripture. Since the Word of the Lord is our spiritual food, we must have a balanced diet and not linger only in the books and passages we love the most.

Adoration. When we are blessed by the Scriptures, we must lift our hearts and worship the Lord. "I will praise You with uprightness of heart, when I learn Your righteous judgments" (Ps. 119:7). The Bible and worship go together (Col. 3:16–17), and as we are filled with the Word of God, we grow in our worship of God. We don't worship the Bible; we worship the God who gave us the Bible.

Application. "Be doers of the word, and not hearers only, deceiving yourselves" (James 1:22). The only Scripture that really goes to work in our lives and helps us grow is that which we obey. We can sit at the dinner table and admire the various foods, but if we don't eat what is set before us, we will never benefit from the meal. It isn't enough to read the recipe. We must chew, swallow, and digest the food, which means reading the Scriptures, meditating on them, and obeying what God tells us to do.

Sanctify them by Your truth. Your word is truth.

John 17:17

53

In all your ways acknowledge Him, and *He shall direct your paths.*

Proverbs 3:5–6 are verses many of us learned early in our Christian life, because if we are to please the Lord, we must walk in his will. I had been saved for about three years when the Lord gave me Psalm 16:11 as my life verse, and it opens with, "You will show me the path of life." The Christian life is a journey, not a parking lot, and we must meet certain conditions if we are to stay on his path and not wander into detours.

We must give him all our heart. The Christian walk is a walk of faith, and we cannot trust or serve two masters. Double-minded people are unstable in all their ways (James 1:6–8). "And you will seek Me and find Me, when you search for Me with all your heart" (Jer. 29:13). How would a prospective bride feel if her fiancé said to her, "I promise to be faithful to you at least eighty percent of the time"? Or how would a diner respond if the server said, "Our water is 90 percent pure"? Total devotion to Christ is not an option; it's essential. We are to love the Lord our God with all our heart (Matt. 22:37). When Jesus called Peter, James, and John, "they forsook all and followed Him" (Luke 5:11).

We must trust him completely. Faith is living without scheming. It's living with the confidence that God means what he says and does what he promises. Some people turn the "big problems" over to the Lord but try to manage the "little matters" by themselves, and soon those "little matters" become "big problems." The will of God comes from the heart of God and is an expression of his love for us individually. "The counsel of the LORD stands forever, the plans of

His heart to all generations" (Ps. 33:11). If we obey him, he delights in us (Ps. 37:23); if we disobey him, he disciplines us (Heb. 12:3–11).

We must not trust ourselves. "Do you see a man wise in his own eyes? There is more hope for a fool than for him" (Prov. 26:12). "He who trusts in his own heart is a fool" (Prov. 28:26). This doesn't mean we shut off our brains and ignore past training and experience, but rather we don't depend on them. "The heart is deceitful above all things, and desperately wicked; who can know it?" (Jer. 17:9). Situations or experiences may be similar but they are not identical, and to know the difference we need the discernment that only the Lord can give (James 1:5).

We must seek to glorify God alone. "In all your ways acknowledge Him" (Prov. 3:6). That means that our purpose in life is to glorify God and not magnify ourselves. "Therefore, whether you eat or drink, or whatever you do, do all to the glory of God" (1 Cor. 10:31). If we trust and obey, the Lord will never lead us where his grace cannot help us honor him. We must examine our motives carefully to discern whether we are pleasing ourselves or pleasing the Lord, and sometimes this requires us to take extra time in the Word of God and in prayer. When we are in God's will, we can give thanks for everything (1 Thess. 5:18), for walking on the difficult paths of life often glorifies Jesus the most.

Yes, we may gather information, counsel with spiritual people, pray, meditate on God's Word, and make decisions. But we must remember what Solomon wrote: "A man's heart plans his way, but the LORD directs his steps" (Prov. 16:9). We must be open to the Lord and ready to make changes as he leads us.

> O LORD, I know the way of man is not in himself;
> It is not in man who walks to direct his own steps.
>
> Jeremiah 10:23

54

Wisdom is the principal thing; therefore get wisdom. And in all your getting, get understanding.

PROVERBS 4:7

The English word "principal" comes from the Latin *primus*, which means "first." Wisdom is the first thing, the most important thing, the supreme thing. Why? Wisdom is supreme because *it touches every area of life*. In the book of Proverbs, Solomon shows us that wisdom is needed in the home, in the neighborhood, on the job, in marriage, in raising children, in earning money and spending it, and in our walk with the Lord. Wisdom is to the mind what courage is to the heart and will. Of what value is a strong, skillful body if we don't have the courage to do the work or fight the battle? But what good is it to have knowledge, training, experience, and opportunities if we don't have the wisdom to use them properly? "The fear of the LORD is the beginning of wisdom, and the knowledge of the Holy One is understanding" (Prov. 9:10).

Wisdom is supreme because *it transforms learning into living*. Of what profit is a good education, even an education in the Bible, if we don't know how to put it into practice? It's embarrassing to have a reputation for "brains" and constantly make a mess out of life. I have a book in my library entitled *Why Smart People Do Dumb Things*. Why do they do it? One reason is because they lack wisdom! Christians are supposed to be disciples, and perhaps the nearest equivalent to "disciple" is *apprentice*. Apprentices learn by listening to the instructor, watching the instructor at work, and then doing the work as the instructor watches them. We can watch Olympic swimmers, read books on swimming, and hear lectures on swimming, but eventually we have to dive into the pool and swim! Too many professed Christians are good at listening to and learning from the Bible but very weak when it comes to obeying what it says. True disciples trust the Holy Spirit to give them wisdom to put into practice what they learn. They aren't just listeners and readers; they are doers.

Wisdom is supreme because *it transforms living into learning*. Life becomes a school and not just a series of events, for godly wisdom transforms events into experience and experience into character. Far too many Christians go through life never learning from joy or sorrow, pain or pleasure, success or failure. How tragic to come to the end of life and discover we had not really lived! British novelist and critic Aldous Huxley said, "Experience is not what happens to a man. Experience is what a man does with what happens to him." Events are what you write about in your journal. Experience is what God writes on your heart as a result of these events. Ralph Waldo Emerson wrote, "Life is a series of lessons which must be lived to be understood."

Wisdom is supreme because *it opens the way to godly living*. Wisdom is an attribute of God. "Oh, the depth of the riches both of the wisdom and knowledge of God" (Rom. 11:33). The Holy Spirit is the Spirit of wisdom (Isa. 11:2), and Jesus Christ *is* the wisdom of God (1 Cor. 1:24; Col. 2:3). Smart people can acquire money, power, and prestige, and God can use these things; but wise people go beyond them and grow in spiritual wealth and power to the glory of God. Our world is filled with knowledge, but "the wisdom of this world is foolishness with God" (1 Cor. 3:19). Life is short and it moves swiftly, so we must begin early to learn wisdom.

> Teach us to number our days,
> That we may gain a heart of wisdom.
>
> Psalm 90:12

115

55

Keep my commands and live, and my law as the apple of your eye.

There are many reasons why we should obey God's commands, but the main reason is that we might please God and glorify his name. "I always do those things that please Him," Jesus said (John 8:29). It's a wonderful day in a home when the children obey because they love their parents and want to please them. If we want God's best blessing in our lives, we must give him our best as we learn God's Word and obey it. Consider the benefits.

Obedience sustains life. Each of us is building a life, and every building needs a strong and lasting foundation. According to Jesus, obedience is the only foundation that will last (Matt. 7:24–27). Halfhearted Christians fall to pieces when the storms of life begin to blow, but wholehearted, obedient Christians outlast the storms. God doesn't promise us easy lives, but he does promise us his presence and his care no matter what may happen. According to Nehemiah 1:5, God keeps his covenant and mercy with those who love him and obey his commandments.

Obedience makes the Bible more precious to us. It becomes as "the apple of our eye." This refers to the pupil of the eye and stands for anything that is precious and irreplaceable (Deut. 32:10; Zech. 2:8). Disobedient Christians have no pleasure in reading the Scriptures and meditating on them because the Spirit cannot instruct them, but the obedient child of God finds great delight in the Word of God (Ps. 1:1–2). One of the keys to Bible knowledge is a willingness to obey what God teaches us (John 7:17). Unbelievers or disobedient believers may learn the facts of the Bible, but they cannot learn the deeper truths that God wants us to learn.

Obedience enriches and fulfills life. There's a great difference between making a living and making a life, and the Lord wants us to achieve both. He has a life plan for each of us (Eph. 2:10) and will work out that plan if we obey him (Rom. 12:1–2). Joshua is a good example of this truth. He began as a soldier (Exod. 17:8–16) and then became an assistant to Moses (Exod. 24:13; Num. 11:28). He was one of the spies who explored Canaan (Num. 13) and with Caleb encouraged the people to trust God and enter the land. Then he became successor to Moses and led the nation into Canaan and conquered the land (Deut. 31:1–8). Every one of us should read Joshua 1:1–9 and obey these divine principles for effective leadership.

Obedience keeps us close to God and rewards life. We are united to Christ as branches in a vine (John 15:1–8) and members of a body (1 Cor. 12), and this union is the basis for communion. The secret of fruit-bearing, effective service is found in communion, abiding in Christ (John 15:1–17). From the world's viewpoint, the obedient Christian is a loser, deprived of all that the world has to offer; but just the opposite is true. The obedient Christian enjoys blessings from the Lord that the world can neither see nor experience. "If anyone loves Me, he will keep My word," Jesus said, "and My Father will love him, and We will come to him and make Our home with him" (John 14:23). The apostle John wrote that "whoever keeps His word, truly the love of God is perfected in him" (1 John 2:5). No matter what trials or challenges come to obedient believers, they enjoy peace and confidence, knowing that suffering will one day be transformed into glory (1 Pet. 4:12–19). If we are "doing the will of God from the heart" (Eph. 6:6), it will be worth it all when we see Jesus.

Only be strong and very courageous, that you may observe to do according to all the law which Moses My servant commanded you; do not turn from it to the right hand or to the left, that you may prosper wherever you go.

Joshua 1:7

56

Wisdom has built her house, she has hewn out her seven pillars.

PROVERBS 9:1

Many times in Scripture we find the Lord offering people two choices, and those choices are also before us today and every day. Moses wrote, "I have set before you life and death, blessing and cursing" (Deut. 30:19). Jesus pictured a broad, easy way that leads to destruction and a narrow way that leads to life (Matt. 7:13–14). In Proverbs 9, Solomon introduces us to two women, Wisdom and Folly, and urges us to accept Wisdom's invitation, for Folly's house is the way to death and hell. There is quite a contrast between these two women!

Wisdom builds but Folly destroys. Wisdom lives in a beautiful mansion and she invites us to a sumptuous banquet, but Folly invites us to a meal of bread and water (v. 17) in a common house that is a doorway to death (v. 18). Folly has nothing to offer but sinful pleasures that last a few moments but result in eternal judgment. All of us are builders, and we get the blueprints and materials for building our life either from Wisdom or Folly. Paul told young Timothy that "godliness is profitable for all things, having promise of the life that now is and of that which is to come" (1 Tim. 4:8). Jesus promised, "But seek first the kingdom of God and His righteousness, and all these things shall be added to you" (Matt. 6:33). I am grateful to God for all those who helped to "build me" and who encouraged me to secure my blueprints and materials from Wisdom. The building process isn't over yet, and daily I pray that God will help me to end well.

Wisdom speaks truth but Folly lies. The sunshine of truth shines on Wisdom's mansion, while fog and darkness enshroud Folly's hovel. Lies always lead to bondage. Sir Walter Scott wrote, "O what a tangled web we weave / When first we practice to deceive." The truth sets us free (John 8:32). Christian students in secular schools must especially beware of "scientific truths" or "historical truths" that are really lies when measured by the Bible. Godly Scottish pastor Robert Murray M'Cheyne wrote to such a student, "Beware of the atmosphere of the classics. . . . True, we ought to know them, but only as a chemist handles poisons—to discover their qualities, not to infect their blood with them." Years ago a godly evangelist said to me, "Study all you can, but put it under the blood of Christ and let him tell you how to use it."

Wisdom nourishes us but Folly starves us or poisons us. Wisdom spreads her table with meat, wine, and bread, while Folly mentions only stolen bread and water. Starting with the Bible and the hymnal, there is a wealth of wisdom available to us from Christian writers and we ought to take advantage of it. I especially appreciate the biographies and autobiographies of outstanding Christian men and women. I also enjoy reading their letters. Folly says her food is "sweet and pleasant" (v. 17), but she doesn't tell you that in the end it becomes poison (v. 18)! My doctor says, "You are what you eat," but we also are what we read and think about. "For as he thinks in his heart, so is he" (Prov. 23:7).

Make the right choice. Sit at Wisdom's table, open your Bible, read it, and meditate on it. The inspired Scriptures always come first. But there are also helpful books by gifted Christians, so open one of them and nourish your mind and heart on the truth God has shared with the author. God has often taught me just what I needed to know as I studied the pages of a book that magnified Jesus Christ and opened up spiritual truth. I trust that will also happen to you.

> You are my portion, O LORD;
> I have said that I would keep Your words.
>
> Psalm 119:57

57

Hatred stirs up strife, *but love covers all sins.*

PROVERBS 10:12

As wonderful as love is, there are some things it cannot do. It cannot *condone* sin because sin is an offense against a holy and loving God. Love cannot *cleanse* sin because "the blood of Jesus Christ His Son cleanses us from all sin" (1 John 1:7). But love can and should *cover* sin so that we don't gossip and bring disgrace to the name of the Lord. We should be overcomers.

We should overcome evil with good. "Do not be overcome by evil, but overcome evil with good" (Rom. 12:21). Shem and Japheth obeyed this command when they covered their drunken father Noah's naked body and were careful not to look at him. Their brother Ham had looked upon Noah and told his brothers about it, but he himself had done nothing to remedy the situation. "A fool's wrath is known at once, but a prudent man covers shame" (Prov. 12:16). The law of Moses had not yet been given, but surely there was something in the heart of Ham that could have prompted him to do the right thing. When he reported the scene to his brothers, was he weeping or jesting? Edmund Burke said, "All that is necessary for evil to triumph is that good men do nothing," and James wrote, "Therefore, to him who knows to do good and does not do it, to him it is sin" (James 4:17).

We must overcome lies with truth. The classic example of this is the way Joseph dealt with his deceitful brothers who sold him into slavery and lied to their father by claiming he had been slain by a wild beast (Gen. 37:12–35). God was with Joseph in his trials and eventually made him second ruler of Egypt. When, during the famine, his brothers came to Egypt to buy food, Joseph dealt with them sternly *because he loved them* and wanted to see them set free from their guilt. He spoke the truth in love (Eph. 4:15), for truth without love is brutality and love without truth is hypocrisy. Joseph had paid a great price in Egypt, so their deliverance was not cheap. His brothers had to feel the painful consequences of their lies before they could enjoy forgiveness.

We must overcome hatred with love. Again, I think of Joseph, whose brothers hated him (Gen. 37:1–11). But Joseph bore no ill will toward them and eventually his love won out. I think also of David, who had opportunities to destroy King Saul but instead spared him and would not even allow anyone to speak disrespectfully of him. "He who covers a transgression seeks love" (Prov. 17:9). The apostle Peter quotes our text in his first letter: "And above all things have fervent love for one another, for 'love will cover a multitude of sins'" (1 Pet. 4:8). When you read David's lament over Saul's death, you find him praising Saul and not naming his sins (2 Sam. 1:17–27).

Of course, the greatest example of "covering love" is seen in our Lord Jesus Christ. Consider how he "covered" the sins of Judas and gave him opportunities to change. (Had Peter known Judas's plans, he might have drawn his sword!) After his resurrection, Jesus met privately with Peter and forgave him (Luke 24:34; 1 Cor. 15:5), and later Jesus restored Peter publicly (John 21:15–19). At Pentecost, Peter's preaching brought three thousand people into the kingdom.

"A new commandment I give to you, that you love one another," Jesus told his disciples (John 13:34), and Paul wrote, "he who loves another has fulfilled the law" (Rom. 13:8). Love is not only the greatest commandment, but it is also the greatest covering. We are never closer to the Lord than when we love others and practice forgiveness.

The fruit of the Spirit is love.

Galatians 5:22

58

A true witness delivers souls, but a deceitful witness speaks lies.

The court system in Israel was far from perfect and often the prophets had to warn the people against bribery and perjury (Isa. 1:23; Amos 5:12; Micah 7:3). The book of Proverbs warns that deceitful witnesses will be punished and might even perish for their evil deeds (19:5, 9; 21:28). When we move our text out of the courtroom and into everyday life, and make God's people the witnesses, it throws new light on the seriousness of sharing the gospel with others.

A tragedy. It is certainly tragic when an innocent person is punished or even killed because somebody told lies on the witness stand *while a true witness said nothing.* But this could happen many times in the course of a day when you and I fail to use the opportunities the Lord gives us to share Christ with others. There are times when "silence is golden," but there are also times when silence is cowardly. We need to be like the apostles who boldly told the religious leaders, "We cannot but speak the things which we have seen and heard" (Acts 4:20). How many "nice people" do we know who are not born again because nobody has told them how to be saved? Does our disobedience bother us?

An opportunity. We don't just "witness" to lost souls; we seek to deliver them from bondage. It's a patient ministry of love. We today are not official apostles, but the Lord has given us the same opportunity he gave Paul, "to open their eyes in order to turn them from darkness to light, and from the power of Satan to God, that they may receive forgiveness of sins and an inheritance among those who are sanctified by faith in Me" (Acts 26:18). The lost are bound in sin, blind, and living in mental, moral, and spiritual darkness; slaves of Satan, guilty of disobedience, and bankrupt of the spiritual riches you and I have in Christ. They don't need prosecuting attorneys, they need witnesses! Arguing religion with people and debating points of theology is not witnessing. People can argue with us about churches and theology *but not about our personal witness about what Christ has done for us*! The blind beggar that Jesus healed had it right: "One thing I know: that though I was blind, now I see" (John 9:25).

A necessity. The essential element in witnessing is truth. Like a witness in court, I must tell (and live) "the truth, the whole truth, and nothing but the truth, so help me God." And he will help me! "You shall receive power when the Holy Spirit has come upon you; and you shall be witnesses to Me" (Acts 1:8). The Holy Spirit is the Spirit of truth (John 14:17) and the Scriptures are the Word of truth (Eph. 1:13); if we are walking in the truth (3 John 3–4), the Lord will give us the ability to bear witness of Jesus. The faith walk and work of a humble child of God is as much part of witnessing as the words we speak and the Bible verses we quote. It is the *true* witness who delivers souls, not the angry debater or the peddler with a memorized sales pitch. True witnesses speak God's truth in love, listen in love, and trust the Spirit to work. Wanted: true witnesses!

> Deliver those who are drawn toward death,
> And hold back those stumbling to the slaughter.
> If you say, "Surely we did not know this,"
> Does not He who weighs the hearts consider it?
> He who keeps your soul, does He not know it?
> And will He not render to each man according to his
> deeds?
>
> Proverbs 24:11–12

123

59

The fear of the LORD is the instruction of wisdom,
and before honor is humility.

PROVERBS 15:33

ndrew Murray said that humility is not thinking meanly of ourselves but simply not thinking of ourselves at all. Humility is the grace that, when we know we have it, we have lost it. God hates pride (Prov. 6:16–17) and we should hate it too, especially in ourselves (Prov. 8:13). To better understand honor and humility, let's look at four persons found in biblical history.

King Saul—from honor to humiliation. Almost everybody admired Saul when he was made king of Israel. He was tall, strong, and apparently humble (1 Sam. 9:21), but in the years that followed, pride possessed him and he became envious, suspicious, and vindictive, what we today would call a control freak. He began in great honor but ended in greater humiliation because the Lord abandoned him. Instead of seeking God's will, he visited a witch to get guidance for a battle; and he ended up committing suicide on the battlefield (1 Sam. 28:3–25; 31:1–6). Had he humbled himself before God and listened to the prophet Samuel, matters would have been different.

King David—from humility to honor. Even as a very young man, David was submitted to the Lord, to his father, to his brothers in Saul's army, and to King Saul. God honored David by giving him victory over a lion, a bear, and the giant Goliath. As Saul's aide, David played the harp to help Saul get over his restless spirit. When David was an officer in Saul's army, he won so many battles that the people sang his praises and Saul became envious and tried to kill him. For perhaps ten years, David led his own small army as he waited for the Lord

124

to give him the throne of Israel. He was a humble young man (Ps. 131) and God honored him when the time was right (Ps. 78:67–72). "Therefore humble yourselves under the mighty hand of God, that He may exalt you in due time" (1 Pet. 5:6).

Absalom—from pride to great dishonor. Absalom was one of David's sons, a handsome man with a winning personality and great ambition. But he was also a proud man with no faith in God. Absalom was popular, what today we would call a celebrity, but he had no character and used people to accomplish his own selfish purposes. More than anything else, he wanted to be king and was even willing to attack his own father to gain the crown. "God resists the proud, but gives grace to the humble" (1 Pet. 5:5–7; *see* Prov. 3:34). Unwisely, David wanted his army to spare his son, but God willed otherwise and Absalom was caught in the boughs of a tree by his thick hair and stabbed to death by Joab, commander of David's army. Absalom's body was thrown into a pit and buried under a heap of rocks, a monument to his arrogance and folly.

Jesus—humbled and honored. Two words summarize the evidence for our Lord's humility: sacrifice and service. Jesus "made Himself of no reputation. . . . He humbled Himself and became obedient to the point of death, even the death of the cross. Therefore God has highly exalted Him" (Phil. 2:7–9). His birth was humble and so was his life. He had no home and was at everybody's beck and call morning and night. "But he who is greatest among you shall be your servant," he told his disciples. "And whoever exalts himself will be humbled, and he who humbles himself will be exalted" (Matt. 23:11–12). Humility is the "soil" in which all the other Christian graces must grow and bear fruit, while pride is the "soil" that produces the noxious weeds of sin. Today Jesus is enthroned far above every power and every name (Eph. 1:20–23). The humble, suffering servant is King of Kings and Lord of Lords!

60

A *merry heart does good*, like medicine, but a broken spirit dries the bones.

PROVERBS 17:22

Let's ask some questions of our text and discover what practical help it will give us.

Why the heart? The emphasis in the book of Proverbs is on *wisdom*; in the Hebrew text, the words *wise* and *wisdom* are used nearly one hundred times. But the word *heart* is also found nearly one hundred times! Most people connect wisdom with the education of the mind, but the Bible connects wisdom with both the mind and the heart. Education is learning, but wisdom is applying learning and experiencing success. "The wise in heart will receive commands" (Prov. 10:8); "The wise in heart will be called prudent" (Prov. 16:21). It isn't enough to learn truth; we must also love both truth and wisdom. Knowing facts from the Bible isn't the same as receiving the deeper truths that reveal God's wisdom. "Has not God made foolish the wisdom of this world?" (1 Cor. 1:20). Solomon's many wives and concubines turned his heart away from the Lord (1 Kings 11:3–4), and he forgot that he had written "Keep your heart with all diligence, for out of it spring the issues of life" (Prov. 4:23). Our lives flow out of the abundance of the heart (Matt. 12:34), and if we don't diligently guard the heart, we will not learn God's wisdom.

Why a merry heart? What makes people happy tells a great deal about their character and ambitions. But happiness isn't something we seek, it's a byproduct of doing the will of God. If we walk with the Lord and obey him, the Spirit will give us a joyful heart, and "the joy of the LORD is your strength" (Neh. 8:10). Our outlook often determines our outcome, and starting the day with a negative attitude can rob us of

God's best blessing. "The fruit of the Spirit is love, joy, [and] peace" (Gal. 5:22). True joy in the Lord does not depend on perfect circumstances or the absence of cares. Paul and Silas were joyful in a prison (Acts 16:25), and Jesus sang a hymn before he went to the garden to be arrested (Matt. 26:30). God doesn't always replace pain and burdens with joy; his usual way is to *transform* the pain and burdens into joy! The same baby that gives the travailing mother pain, when delivered, also gives her joy (John 16:20–24).

What good comes from it all? "A merry heart does good, like medicine," Solomon wrote (Prov. 17:22). It isn't the prescription that changes us, it's taking the medication. "He sent His word and healed them" (Ps. 107:20). God's chastening isn't immediately joyous, but afterward it produces "peaceable fruit" (Heb. 12:11). Meditate on the Word, pray, and fellowship with praying people, and the joy of the Lord will get into your system and start healing your heart. God is not glorified by critical, sulky, and complaining Christians. He is glorified by believers who accept his will and find in it the healing joy of his grace. Paul's letter to the Philippians is saturated with joy, yet he wrote it from confinement in Rome, awaiting a trial that might lead to his execution!

How do we begin? We begin by taking our eyes off of ourselves and our circumstances and fixing them by faith on Jesus (Heb. 12:1–2). We stop sulking and complaining and start devoting time to meditating on the Scriptures and letting God's promises saturate us with "medicine." The heart of every problem is the problem in the heart. If we ask, the Lord can restore to us the joy of his salvation (Ps. 51:12). There is no substitute for simply waiting on the Lord and resting on his promises.

> Commit your way to the LORD,
> Trust also in Him,
> And He shall bring it to pass.
>
> Psalm 37:5

61

> The sluggard says, "There is a lion outside;
> I will be killed in the streets!"
>
> ━━━━━ ✦ **PROVERBS 22:13 NASB**

lothful and *sluggard* are old words that describe lazy people. *Slothful* comes from the slow-moving sloth in the animal word and *sluggard* from the slower-moving slug in the world of mollusks. Other words we might use today would be loafer, slouch, or goldbricker.

Sluggards are lazy. If there is one person Solomon could not stand it was the lazy man or woman who refused to carry their weight on the job—or didn't even show up! The people in the Bible whom God blessed and used were all workers. In fact, many of them were working when the Lord called them. Moses and David were both tending sheep; Gideon was threshing wheat; Isaiah was worshiping in the temple; and Peter, Andrew, James, and John were fishing. In his parable of the talents, Jesus called the servant with one talent wicked, lazy, and unprofitable because he refused to put himself and his one talent to work (Matt. 25:14–30). Paul commanded God's people in Rome to be "not lagging in diligence, fervent in spirit, serving the Lord" (Rom. 12:11), and he told the servants in the Colossian church, "whatever you do, do it heartily, as to the Lord and not to men" (Col. 3:23).

Sluggards are liars. It's not likely there was a lion in the street, and even if there were, the man and his neighbors could have driven it away or killed it. David was only a teenager, yet he killed a lion and a bear that attacked his flock (1 Sam. 17:33–37), and years later, one of his top soldiers killed a lion in "a pit on a snowy day" (2 Sam. 23:20). The sluggard was only making an excuse, and people who are good at making excuses are usually not good at doing anything else. American evangelist Billy Sunday defined an excuse as "the skin of a reason stuffed with a lie." The lazy person doesn't plow because it's too cold outside (Prov. 20:4), and when harvest time arrives, he has nothing to harvest (Prov. 24:30–34). Instead of making excuses, he should have been confessing his sins and asking the Lord to help him be a faithful worker.

Sluggards are losers. Not only do sluggards lose their harvest (income), which would certainly affect their household, but they also lose the benefits that come to the body and soul of the faithful worker. Work is not punishment for sin, because our first parents worked in the garden before sin came on the scene (Gen. 2:15). Work is a privilege and an opportunity for us to learn and grow, to use our God-given abilities and the natural resources the Lord has given us so that we may provide for ourselves and others and give to the Lord (Eph. 4:28). Employment ought to bring us enjoyment and enrichment (2 Tim. 2:17), even though we are weary at the close of day. But that's why God provided sleep! Jesus was so weary in ministry that he went to sleep in a boat on a stormy sea. "The sleep of a laboring man is sweet" (Eccles. 5:12). To be a sluggard in matters material or spiritual (Heb. 6:12) is to forfeit the blessings God has for us.

Sluggards are not leaders. The men and women who helped to make civil and religious history were people who sacrificed and served and didn't make excuses. If you need stirring up, read Paul's brief autobiography in 2 Corinthians 11:22–33! Jesus prayed early in the morning and he labored all the day and into the night hours—and he is our example. Yes, he took time off with his disciples, but that was so they could regain the strength to serve more.

I agree with Dr. Bob Cook, who said, "Hard work is a thrill and a joy, when you are in the will of God."

Go to the ant, you sluggard!
Consider her ways and be wise.

Proverbs 6:6–7

62

To everything there is a season, *a time for every purpose* under heaven.

ECCLESIASTES 3:1

W hen Adam and Eve named their second son Abel, they gave King Solomon the key word for Ecclesiastes; the Hebrew word *hebel* means "vanity," a word used in Ecclesiastes thirty-eight times. Solomon examined many different aspects of life to find out if life was worth living, and the more he pondered, the more he concluded that life had no meaning. It was vanity. As early as the second chapter, he said, "Therefore I hated life" (2:17), quite a statement for a man who knew much and had everything. Occasionally we may feel that way, especially when we read or watch the news or when some dream plan of ours becomes a nightmare. But our text shares three truths that encourage us to take a more positive view of life.

In life we experience a sequence of events. Solomon calls them "seasons" and "times." Ecclesiastes has forty instances of the word "time." God dwells in eternity and has put eternity in our hearts (3:11), which explains our deep dissatisfaction with "things" and "events" and our craving for something more. That "something more" is what Jesus called abundant life (John 10:10), and it is found only when we trust him as Savior and serve him as Lord. Solomon does write about enjoying life (Eccles. 2:24; 3:12–15, 22; 5:18–20; 8:15; 9:7–10), but it's strictly on the human plane: enjoy your work, enjoy food and drink, and enjoy your spouse and family. But an unsaved pagan can do all that! As good as these things are, we want something more in life, something that will prepare us for death and eternity. Solomon often mentions death, and the only true preparation for death is knowing Jesus Christ (John 11:25–26).

These events help to accomplish God's purposes. Capable scientists and historians have attempted to discover purpose in the universe and in human history but so far have failed, primarily because God has been left out of the equation. We are creatures of time and see only the sequence of events. It's like looking at three pieces of a jigsaw puzzle and trying to imagine the whole picture. God sees the whole picture and this earth is the "theater" of the universe where he is working out his purposes and revealing his plans. "The earth is the LORD's . . . the world and those who dwell therein" (Ps. 24:1). There are times in our lives when we wonder what God is doing, but we can claim Romans 8:28 and know that all that is happening is working out for our good and his glory. "He has made everything beautiful in its time" (Eccles. 3:11). In this life, Christians live on promises, not explanations. The explanations will come when this life ends and we enter eternity. What Jesus said to Peter can be applied to us today: "What I am doing you do not understand now, but you will know after this" (John 13:7). When we pray, "Your will be done on earth as it is in heaven," we are asking for fulfillment and not explanations or reasons.

God's purposes come from his loving heart. Ponder Psalm 33:10–11 and rejoice. The Lord has purposes for nations as well as for individuals; his purposes come from his heart *and they will be fulfilled!* Every believer can say, "The LORD will perfect that which concerns me; your mercy, O LORD, endures forever. Do not forsake the works of Your hands" (Ps. 138:8). Our problem is that we are in a hurry to get our will done right now instead of being willing to wait on the Lord. Abraham and Sarah waited twenty-five years for their promised son, Isaac, and Joseph waited thirteen years to become the second ruler of Egypt, and both were expressions of God's love and fulfillment of his wise plan.

Wait, I say, on the LORD!

Psalm 27:14

63

Wash yourselves, make yourselves clean; put away
the evil of your doings from before My eyes.

We're accustomed to asking the Lord to wash us
after we have sinned (Ps. 51:2, 7), but this text
commands us to wash *ourselves*! This doesn't
mean that we have the authority and ability to remove our
own sins, but rather that we need to repent and put out of our
lives the things that make it easy for us to sin. I heard about a
church member who prayed long at each prayer meeting and
always closed by saying, "And, Lord, take the cobwebs out
of my life." One of the men in the group had gotten weary
of hearing this and one night called out, "And, Lord, while
you're at it, *kill the spider*!" That's what this text means.

Sin will defile us. Sin is pictured in many ways in Scripture—darkness, disease, bondage, and even death—but one
of the most familiar is defilement. The law of Moses taught
the Jewish people to distinguish between the clean and the
unclean, not only in foods but also in the contacts of daily life.
For example, it was defiling to touch a dead body or a person
who had a running sore. These rules helped keep the people
healthy but also reminded them to keep their lives clean so
they could enjoy God's blessings. If the priests on duty in the
sanctuary failed to keep clean, they might die (Exod. 30:17–21).
We may not take our sinning as seriously as we should, but the
Lord can see the defilement in our hearts. "If I regard iniquity
in my heart, the Lord will not hear" (Ps. 66:18). Nobody on
earth is sinless, but we ought to strive to be as clean as possible
before the Lord. First John 1:5–10 calls this walking in the light.

Religion can disguise us. To try to hide our sins from the
Lord and others is only to add another sin to the record:

hypocrisy. When you read Isaiah 1, you see the sad picture of sinful people crowding into the temple, offering sacrifices to God, lifting their hands and praying—and then going out of the temple and sinning again and again. They faithfully observed the Jewish holy days. They were certain that their prayers and sacrifices would please the Lord and give others the impression that they were godly people. But they were wrong. We certainly can't fool God with our religious rituals, and even if we fool our friends, it does no good. Eventually the truth comes out, and even if our secret sins are not exposed, we have still alienated ourselves from the Lord and are walking in darkness.

Only God can deliver us. His invitation is "Come now" and his promise is "Though your sins are like scarlet, they shall be as white as snow. Though they are red like crimson, they shall be as wool" (Isa. 1:18). God forgives our sins, but he also commands us to forsake the things that encourage us to sin. "Let the wicked forsake his way" (55:7) and start walking in the right way with the right people. To obey this command, some Christians must clean out their library and magazine rack, and perhaps their music collection. "Therefore, having these promises, beloved, let us cleanse ourselves from all filthiness of the flesh and spirit, perfecting holiness in the fear of God" (2 Cor. 7:1). Note the once-for-all crisis ("cleanse ourselves") and the process that follows ("perfecting holiness"). "[Lay] aside all malice, all deceit, hypocrisy, envy, and all evil speaking" (1 Pet. 2:1).

We must wash ourselves and make ourselves clean as proof that we are serious about living a holy life. God will renew us if we will repent and put away the sins that defile us.

> Draw near to God and He will draw near to you. Cleanse your hands, you sinners; and purify your hearts, you double-minded.
>
> James 4:8

133

64

Take heed, and be quiet; do not fear or be faint-hearted for these two stubs of smoking firebrands, for the fierce anger of Rezin and Syria, and the son of Remaliah.

ISAIAH 7:4

A time of fear. Ahaz, king of Judah, was in a very difficult situation. King Rezin of Syria and King Pekah of Israel had conspired to attack Judah and put another king on the throne. But the temple and priesthood were in Judah, and Ahaz belonged to the dynasty of David from which the promised Messiah would come. "So his heart and the heart of his people were moved as the trees of the woods are moved with the wind" (v. 2). Whenever we are afraid, it's wise to open the Scriptures, listen to the Lord, and get his point of view. God didn't see Rezin and Pekah as terrible blazing torches but only as pitiful stubs about to go out. When Moses sent the spies into the land of Canaan, ten of the spies gave an accurate description of the land *but left God out of the picture!* Two of the spies, Caleb and Joshua, saw the land from God's point of view and encouraged the people to enter the land and claim their inheritance. The ten unbelieving spies died, and during the next thirty-eight years of Israel's wandering, every Israelite who had been twenty years of age and older died in the wilderness except Caleb and Joshua. Unbelief is a dangerous sin (Num. 13–14).

A time for faith. Getting God's point of view means walking by faith. "You will keep him in perfect peace, whose mind is stayed on You, because he trusts in You" (Isa. 26:3). But we must not be double-minded by seeking God's help and then depending on our own schemes (James 1:5–8); we must wholly trust in the Lord. Faith is living without scheming.

However, King Ahaz had secretly made a treaty with the king of Assyria, asking his help if Judah was attacked (2 Kings 16:5–9). "Some trust in chariots, some trust in horses, but we will remember the name of the LORD our God" (Ps. 20:7). One of God's names is *Jehovah Nissi*, which means "The Lord Is My Banner." It commemorates the first battle Israel won after they had come out of Egypt (Exod. 17:15–16). If we would only remember what the Lord has done for us in the past, it would encourage us to put our trust in him today. Sometimes we have to say with the distraught father, "Lord, I believe; help my unbelief!" (Mark 9:24), remembering that Jesus honored even that prayer.

A time for faithfulness. The name of Isaiah's son who accompanied him to see the king was Shear-Jashub, which means "a remnant shall return." The concept of a Jewish remnant of faithful believers runs through the Old Testament from Noah and his family (Gen. 7:23) and Joseph (Gen. 45:7) to Malachi 3:16; and Paul picks it up in Romans 11:5. (*See* Isa. 1:9; 37:31–32; Luke 12:32.) God has never depended on huge numbers to accomplish his will on earth, and you and I today are a part of that remnant of believers. Malachi 3:16–18 clearly describes the remnant as a small group that fears the Lord, fellowships together, prays together, meditates on spiritual matters, ministers to one another, and exercises spiritual discernment as they bear witness to the lost. God's admonition to us is: "Therefore, lift up your prayer for the remnant that is left" (Isa. 37:4).

Instead of being fearful and upset, let's "take heed and be quiet," knowing that the Lord has everything in control.

Aspire to lead a quiet life.

1 Thessalonians 4:11

65

Can a woman forget her nursing child, and not have compassion on the son of her womb? Surely, they may forget, yet *I will not forget you.*

ISAIAH 49:15

The people of Israel had been complaining about their lot in life and were accusing the Lord of forgetting and forsaking them. This is not an unusual response when the going is difficult and our prayers aren't answered, and we can't see a way out. More than once, even the great King David felt deserted. "How long, O LORD? Will You forget me forever?" (Ps. 13:1). Even the sons of Korah, who served in the sanctuary, at times felt deserted. "Why do You hide Your face, and forget our affliction and our oppression?" (Ps. 44:24). But our text makes it clear that our heavenly Father will not desert his children.

God remembers his people. Israel was in difficult circumstances because they had disobeyed the Lord and he was disciplining them. But even that discipline was evidence that he was with them and cared for them. Sometimes we get like sulking children who go around mumbling, "Nobody loves me," and we only make matters worse. When the Bible says that God "remembers" something or someone, it doesn't mean that his mind had moved into dementia and now he had recovered. God is omniscient and can't forget anything. It simply means that he is about to act. He remembered Noah and delivered him from the flood (Gen. 8:1). God remembered Abraham's prayer and delivered Lot from Sodom (19:29). He remembered Rachel's prayers for a son and gave her Joseph (30:22), and he also remembered Hannah's prayers and gave her Samuel (1 Sam. 1:11, 19). God always does the right thing *at the right time*, when his preparations are complete.

God remembers his covenant promises. When the people of Israel were suffering in Egypt, "God heard their groaning, and God remembered His covenant with Abraham, with Isaac, and with Jacob" (Exod. 2:24; *see* 6:5). God's covenants are as faithful and unchanging as God's character, and we can rely on his promises. Our Lord and Savior Jesus Christ is today "the Mediator of the new covenant" (Heb. 12:24) and God's people honor that covenant each time they celebrate the Lord's Supper. It reminds us of the cost of that covenant, the precious blood of Jesus, as well as the promise that we have God's forgiveness and that Jesus is coming again. Each promise the Lord gives us in his Word is founded on what Jesus did for us on the cross!

God does not remember our sins. King David prayed in Psalm 25:7, "Do not remember the sins of my youth, nor my transgressions; according to Your mercy remember me, for Your goodness' sake, O Lord." Satan is the accuser of God's people before God (Rev. 12:10) and his demons like to accuse us in our own minds and hearts; but God's covenant promise is "their sins and their lawless deeds I will remember no more" (Heb. 8:12; 10:17). This means our sins are no longer recorded or held against us. Saved sinners are not like paroled criminals who go back to prison if they commit another crime. *All our sins have been completely forgiven and forgotten* (Col. 2:13–14). If we do sin, we confess it to the Lord and receive cleansing (1 John 1:9). Don't allow the accuser to trouble you (Zech. 3:1–5).

Let us not forget God! Ponder Deuteronomy 8:11; 32:18 and Jeremiah 2:12; 3:21.

> I, even I, am He who blots out your transgressions for
> My own sake;
> And I will not remember your sins.
>
> Isaiah 43:25

66

Return, you backsliding children, and *I will heal your backslidings.*

JEREMIAH 3:22

The prophet Jeremiah ministered in Judah during the last forty years of the kingdom and witnessed the destruction of Jerusalem and the captivity of the people. Had the rulers listened to him and turned to the Lord, these tragic events would have never occurred. But what happened to the people of Judah can also happen to us, so we had better take heed.

We face a dangerous situation. Except for a faithful remnant, the people of Judah were spiritually sick and didn't know it. They were backslidden and distant from God but refused to admit it or do anything about it. Like a contagious physical sickness, spiritual deterioration starts secretly, then there is a gradual decline that leads to collapse. The people openly turned against the Lord, started worshiping idols, and refused to repent and confess their sins. Wanting to please the people, the false prophets assured them that the Lord would never permit the pagan Babylonians to destroy the temple, but they were wrong (Jer. 6:14; 18:11, 22). Not only were both the city and the temple destroyed, but many of the people were taken to Babylon for seventy years of captivity. It's possible for churches and individual Christians today to duplicate the mistakes the people of Judah made. We can close our eyes to our condition, listen to false counsel, and invite the discipline of the Lord.

We hear a gracious invitation. "Return, you backsliding children." In the Hebrew text of Jeremiah, the word translated *return* is used over one hundred times—ten times in chapter 3 alone. People who backslide don't suddenly fall into traps;

they turn their backs on the Lord and gradually move away from his will and his fellowship. The Lord is longsuffering and does not give up on us. He sends us his Word and if necessary uses loving discipline to awaken us to our danger. And if we obey, he forgives and restores us. But if we persist in believing lies ("You can get away with this"), our situation gets worse and then the Lord must deal with us. If we would only stop at the very beginning and realize what our course will do to the heart of Christ, to us and our loved ones, and to the testimony of the Lord, we would immediately confess our sins and turn to the Lord for forgiveness. The longer we wait, the worse it becomes.

We can experience a marvelous transformation. "I will heal your backslidings." What an encouraging promise! What a wonderful day it is when the physician says to us, "We have identified your problem and there is a remedy." Some professed Christians don't want to be healed of their backslidings, and we wonder if they have truly been born again. Holiness doesn't come automatically no matter how hard we try. We must visit the Great Physician, confess our sins to him, and let him cleanse and heal us. Read Psalm 32 if you want to know what happens to people who cover up their backslidings and what blessings they receive when they confess them. "Those who conceal their sins do not prosper, but those who confess and renounce them find mercy" (Prov. 28:13 TNIV).

The Great Physician is always available. His diagnosis is always correct, his treatments always work—and he makes house calls. And by the way, he has already paid the bill.

> Search me, O God, and know my heart;
> Try me, and know my anxieties;
> And see if there is any wicked way in me,
> And lead me in the way everlasting.
>
> Psalm 139:23–24

67

> Thus says the LORD to the men of Judah and Jerusalem: "*Break up your fallow ground*, and do not sow among thorns."

JEREMIAH 4:3

In Scripture, harvesting is the image of "reaping results," good or bad, from what we say and do. The Lord wants fruit in our lives (Gal. 5:22–23) and a "harvest of souls" from our labors (John 4:34–38). William R. Inge, dean of St. Paul's in London (1911–1934), aptly said, "We are always sowing the future, we are always reaping the past." The more you ponder that statement, the more serious it becomes. Jesus seeks "fruit . . . more fruit . . . much fruit" (John 15:1–8).

Successful harvests require preparation. "Fallow ground" is ground that is inactive because it is unimproved. It has not been plowed or seeded, and therefore can produce no harvest. One reason the land is idle is because "the laborers are few" (Luke 10:2); and Luke 9:57–62 tells us why the laborers are few: the people God calls are making excuses! Jesus is looking for laborers, not loiterers who make excuses.

Preparation involves plowing. According to the parable of the sower (Matt. 13:1–9, 18–23), the good seed of the Word enters our hearts only if the soil has been broken up by repentance and confession. Hard hearts cannot receive God's truth, for the devil comes and snatches away the seed. "Sow for yourselves righteousness, reap in mercy; break up your fallow ground, for it is time to seek the LORD, till He comes and rains righteousness on you" (Hosea 10:12). Prepared soil has tremendous potential, but it is tragic how much undeveloped ground there is in our lives.

Plowing demands perseverance. "No one, having put his hand to the plow, and looking back, is fit for the kingdom of

God" (Luke 9:62). If we are faithful in serving, one day "we shall reap if we do not lose heart" (Gal. 6:9). If the plowman repeatedly looked back and thought only of going back, what kind of rows would he plow? Granted, plowing is hard work, but God's calling includes God's enabling. "I can do all things through Christ who strengthens me" (Phil. 4:13). The enemy gives us every excuse for going on comfortable detours, but the Lord by his example and exhortations encourages us to keep working until the work is done.

Perseverance comes from faith. The Lord does not want us to become "sluggish, but [to] imitate those who through faith and patience inherit the promises" (Heb. 6:12). Faith and patience make a wonderful team! In every area of Christian life and service, we must live by faith, and if we do live by faith, we will develop patience. Without patience, we can learn very little and accomplish almost nothing. James reminds us that it is the testing of our faith that produces patience (James 1:4), and he uses the example of the farmer to encourage us. "See how the farmer waits for the precious fruit of the earth, waiting patiently for it until it receives the early and latter rain" (5:7). "We are God's fellow workers" (1 Cor. 3:9), and if we do our part, he will do his part. "For without Me," Jesus said, "you can do nothing" (John 15:5).

Faith comes from living in the Scriptures. "So then faith comes by hearing, and hearing by the word of God" (Rom. 10:17). Read Hebrews 11 and see what God did in and with ordinary people who received his Word and trusted him. As workers, we must live in the Scriptures and allow the Spirit to instruct us and enable us. We enter into the labors of others, and they into our labors (John 4:38), but it is the Lord who gives the harvest.

Behold, I say to you, lift up your eyes and look at the fields, for they are already white for harvest!

John 4:35

68

Inasmuch as *there is none like You*, O LORD (You are great, and Your name is great in might), who would not fear You, O King of the nations? For this is Your rightful due. For among all the wise men of the nations, and in all their kingdoms, *there is none like You.*

JEREMIAH 10:6–7

The Hebrew prophets kept reminding the people of Israel that Jehovah was the only true and living God and the idols of the Gentiles were nothing, and yet Israel repeatedly turned to those idols for help and had to be disciplined by the Lord. People in the early churches were also snared by idols, *and so are believers in churches today*! Unlike the pagan idols, contemporary idols are not ugly and vicious but beautiful and seductive—celebrities, money, power, authority, sex, entertainment, food—but they are still dead substitutes for the living God and are dangerous. Anything in our lives that replaces the Lord and enslaves us, anything for which we sacrifice so we can have the satisfaction they offer, is an idol and must be abandoned. No idol can do for us what the Lord can do through Jesus Christ!

Only the Lord can save us from our sins. "Look to Me, and be saved, all you ends of the earth! For I am God, and there is no other" (Isa. 45:22). One snowy Sunday morning, young Charles Haddon Spurgeon heard a sermon on that text, trusted Christ, and was saved! "Nor is there salvation in any other, for there is no other name under heaven given among men by which we must be saved" (Acts 4:12).

Only the Lord deserves our worship, sacrifice, and service. At the dedication of the temple, King Solomon opened his prayer with these words: "LORD God of Israel, there is no

God in heaven above or on earth below like You" (1 Kings 8:23). Godly Hannah prayed fervently for a son and God granted her request. When she brought young Samuel to the sanctuary and dedicated him to serve God there, she prayed, "My heart rejoices in the LORD; my horn [strength] is exalted in the LORD. . . . No one is holy like the LORD, for there is none besides You, nor is there any rock like our God" (1 Sam. 2:1–2). If we have idols in our hearts, our affection for the Lord and our allegiance to him will be divided and we cannot please him. In Scripture, idolatry is called "playing the harlot" (Ps. 106:39; Hosea 4:12; James 4:4).

Only the Lord can deliver us from bondage. The judgments God sent against the land of Egypt (Exod. 7–12) were directed against the gods of Egypt so that Pharaoh might know there was no God like the Lord (Exod. 8:10). After their deliverance, the Jews sang praises to their great God. "Who is like you, O LORD, among the gods? Who is like You, glorious in holiness, fearful in praises, doing wonders?" (Exod. 15:11). If anyone or anything enters my life and merits that kind of praise, I am involved in idolatry. If I refuse to give to God the glory he deserves, I am involved in idolatry. Read 1 Corinthians 8 and meditate on what Paul wrote.

Only the Lord can build our character and make us like Jesus. The writer of Psalm 115 ridicules idolatry by contrasting the dead idols with the living God, and he gives this warning to us: "Those who make [idols] are like them; so is everyone who trusts in them" (v. 8). *We become like the idols that we worship.* But to be godly is to be "God-like." Who wants to become like a lifeless idol when we can become more like Jesus, our living Lord (2 Cor. 3:18)?

There is no one like Jesus!

Little children, keep yourselves from idols. Amen.

1 John 5:21

69

And the vessel that he made of clay was marred in the hand of the potter; *so he made it again* into another vessel, as it seemed good to the potter to make.

JEREMIAH 18:4

This episode reminds us that we are clay. Life is a gift and death is our earthly destiny. "For dust you are, and to dust you shall return" (Gen. 3:19). Clay is a weak substance but it has potential. Every baby born into this world is weak, and nobody knows what it will become. The clay jar in itself is not valuable, but what it contains may be very valuable; *and we are made in the image of God.* Apart from the Lord, we may never discover our possibilities or achieve our full potential. The weakness of the clay needs the power and wisdom of God.

That reminds us that *God is the potter.* "The LORD God formed man of the dust of the ground" (Gen. 2:7) is the picture of a potter at work. God is sovereign and can plan for us and make of us whatever pleases him. This doesn't mean we are helpless victims in a controlled world, because the Lord has decreed that we cooperate with him as he makes our lives. Jesus said, "O Jerusalem, Jerusalem. . . . How often I wanted to gather your children together . . . but you were not willing" (Luke 13:34). And keep in mind that "God is love" (1 John 4:8); his decrees are evidences of his love for us so that we need never fear the will of God. We don't spin the potter's wheel; we yield to the potter's hands. I've heard people proudly claim to be "self-made," and I've wanted to say to them, "It's nice of you to take the blame." It's much better to be God-made.

The potter's wheel represents human life. God arranges the affairs of life so that we get to know him, ourselves, others, and the opportunities life presents to us. "For we are His workmanship, created in Christ Jesus for good works, which God prepared beforehand that we should walk in them" (Eph. 2:10). As we submit to his will, he prepares us for what he has prepared for us. The clay on the wheel Jeremiah was watching didn't want to cooperate and several times resisted, and the potter could well have taken it from the wheel and thrown it away—but he kept working and "made it again." God never gives up on us. Think about Moses, David, Jonah, Peter, John Mark, and others in Scripture who failed but became successful. The Potter is in charge, and if we yield to him he will see to it that we accomplish what he has planned for us.

Jeremiah's experience helps us understand *what success is*. It has little to do with fame, power, or wealth. Success is surrendering to the Lord and obeying his will (Rom. 12:1–3), permitting him to mold us as he desires. When we fail, we ask him to make us again and we go on serving. *The marred vessel was still in the potter's hands!* God makes us, sin mars us, but the Potter can mend us and keep working on us. A crippled believer asked a pastor, "Why did God make me like this?" The pastor replied, "He didn't make you—*he is making you!*" The potter takes each vessel and puts it into the furnace, where it is carefully hardened and then given a finish. Otherwise, the vessel would not be very useful. We don't enjoy furnaces, but we need them.

The disciple Judas would not submit to the potter and had a shameful death. The religious leaders purchased a "potter's field" with the money Judas gave back to them and made it into a cemetery where strangers could be buried. Had Judas only learned what it meant to submit to the Potter! You will be a success in God's eyes if only you submit to the Potter and believe he can even make you again.

> The Lord will perfect that which concerns me;
> Your mercy, O Lord, endures forever;
> Do not forsake the works of Your hands.
>
> Psalm 138:8

70

> For I know the thoughts that I think toward you,
> says the LORD, thoughts of peace and not of evil,
> to give you *a future and a hope.*

JEREMIAH 29:11

Over the course of their conquest of Jerusalem, the Babylonian army destroyed the city, robbed the temple of its treasures, and took many captives to Babylon. The prophet Jeremiah chose to remain in the ruined city with the people who had been left behind, but he wrote a letter to the exiles to tell them how to act as the people of God in a pagan environment. God's people today are living in a predominantly pagan environment, so we can learn our responsibilities from Jeremiah.

Accept God's will. The false prophets among the Jews in Babylon were telling the people that they would return home with their treasures within two years (Jer. 28:1–11), but Jeremiah told them it would be seventy years (29:10)! As the people looked back, they knew that God had sent his prophets many times to warn them, but they would not listen. They could not change the past, but they could learn from it, confess their sins (vv. 19, 23), and obey God's Word. The word translated *evil* in our text carries the meaning of "harm." God was hurting them, but not harming them. My doctors have occasionally hurt me, but they have never harmed me. For the exiles to sit around and complain and seek vengeance (Ps. 137) would accomplish nothing and only make their lives more miserable. God's people today may be in trouble because of our own sins or perhaps the sins of others, but in either situation we must surrender to God's will. He knows what he is doing, and the safest place in the world is in the will of God. Accept it. He has his people on his mind and in his heart, and wills for them what is best for them.

Obey God's instructions. Jeremiah didn't tell them to organize protests or develop an underground resistance movement, but to live normal lives, raise families, and prepare for the future. He urged them to pray for the city (Jer. 29:7) as well as for themselves (v. 12). Both Paul and Peter gave this admonition to the early church (Rom. 13; 1 Tim. 2:1–4; 1 Pet. 2:13–15), and it should be heeded today. Christians are supposed to be peacemakers, not troublemakers. If trouble comes because we bear witness to Christ, our first obedience is to the Lord (Acts 4:19–20), but even that witness should be given with meekness and love. The Jewish exiles obeyed Jeremiah's counsel. Seventy years later, thousands of them returned to their land, rebuilt Jerusalem and the temple, and repopulated the land. Because they did, we today have the knowledge of the one true and living God, the inspired Scriptures, and the Savior, Jesus Christ.

Believe God's promises. When you know Jesus Christ as Savior and Lord and pay attention to God's Word, you have a future that is secure. When God puts us in the furnace, he keeps his eye on the thermometer and his hand on the thermostat. He knows how much and how long. The Lord would not break his covenants with Abraham, Isaac, Jacob, and David, nor would he forget his promises to the prophets (Jer. 24:6; 30:10–11; 31:10–14). Any person alive has a future until death, but not everybody has a future with hope in it. "For whatever things were written before were written for our learning, that we through the patience and comfort of the Scriptures might have hope" (Rom. 15:4).

The present will be victorious if we live a day at a time, learning from the past, looking toward the future, and obeying God's will. Remember, God thinks about you and has plans for you.

> Blessed be the LORD....There has not failed one word of all His good promise.
>
> 1 Kings 8:56

71

Thus says the LORD: "The people who survived the sword *found grace in the wilderness*—Israel, when I went to give him rest."

The wilderness is the last place you would expect to find grace, unless the Lord is with you; he can use our "wilderness experiences" to teach us some valuable spiritual lessons.

To the people of Israel, the wilderness was *a place of testing*. God led them in the wilderness for forty years, to humble them and test them (Deut. 8:2); and they usually failed the test. He guided them day and night, he provided food and water, and he helped them defeat their enemies—and yet more than once they wanted to go back to the bondage of Egypt. They provoked both God and Moses, and yet the Lord saw them through. That's grace! The Lord knew the hearts of his people, but they didn't know their own hearts, and God's tests helped them to see how needy they were.

The wilderness was *a place of training* for David, Elijah, and John the Baptist. It was in the wilderness that David hid from King Saul (Ps. 63), and there Elijah learned not to run away from responsibility (1 Kings 19). The prophet was weary and hungry, and Jezebel's murderous threat frightened him, but the Lord gave him rest and food and sent him back into the battle. John the Baptist grew up in the wilderness and learned to listen to God (Luke 1:80; Matt. 3:1, 3). It's in the hard places of life that we discover how gracious the Lord is to his servants, no matter how they feel. "Behold, God is my salvation, I will trust and not be afraid" (Isa. 12:2).

For Jesus, the wilderness was *a place of temptation*, but he turned it into a place of triumph (Matt. 4:1–11) where he could commune with the Father (Luke 5:16). He often went into the wilderness to get away from the crowds and have much-needed time for prayer and meditation (Isa. 50:4–5). Do you ever take "blessing breaks" when you get alone and wait quietly before the Lord? I recommend them.

Philip the evangelist was having great meetings in Samaria when the Lord called him to a desert place to share the gospel with one man, and that wilderness became *a place of testimony* (Acts 8:5–8, 26–40). The traveler was a high-ranking official in Ethiopia, apparently a proselyte to the Jewish faith, and Philip introduced him to the Savior. Paul and Silas had a similar experience in a jail in Philippi as they prayed and worshiped, and the keeper of the prison was converted along with his family and probably some other prisoners (Acts 16:25–34). Praising the Lord in times of "wilderness," pain, and trial can open doors and hearts and give us a harvest. Speaking of Paul, in listing his trials he reminds us that he faced "perils in the wilderness" (2 Cor. 11:26). He doesn't explain what these perils were, but travel was neither safe nor comfortable in those days, and Paul did a lot of traveling.

The world system today is a vast wasteland that doesn't make our pilgrim journey easy. Peter describes the world as "a dark place," and the word translated *dark* means "dirty, murky, miserable, squalid," like a dangerous swamp (2 Pet. 1:19). But we have the Word of God that shines in this dark and dismal world and shows us the way, just as the cloud and fire guided the way for Israel. *Pay close attention to the Scriptures and the world cannot lead you astray.* The wasteland will become a wonderland as God pours out his grace upon you.

> Your word is a lamp to my feet
> And a light to my path.
>
> Psalm 119:105

72

> This is the covenant that I will make with the
> house of Israel after those days, says the LORD:
> I will put My law in their minds, and write it on
> their hearts; and *I will be their God*, and they
> shall be My people.
>
> JEREMIAH 31:33

To think that the great and holy God is willing to be *our* God and share his truth with us as his Spirit writes it in our minds and hearts is something that should overwhelm us and make us thankful, joyful, and obedient. Just consider who this God is!

He is the God of love (2 Cor. 13:11). The pagan nations manufactured gods that commanded worshipers to offer their children on their altars, but our God sent his only Son, as a baby, to grow up and be the sacrifice for our sins. He welcomed the children and took them in his arms and blessed them (Matt. 19:13–15). Jesus loves and welcomes sinners who come to him to be saved (Luke 19:10). God's love is a great love (Eph. 2:4).

He is the God of all grace (1 Pet. 5:10). God in his grace gives us what we don't deserve, and we receive his grace by faith so we can serve him and do good works. "By the grace of God I am what I am," Paul wrote (1 Cor. 15:10), and God said to Paul, "My grace is sufficient for you" (2 Cor. 12:9). His grace is also sufficient for us!

He is the "God who alone is wise" (1 Tim. 1:17). Our world is in the midst of a "knowledge explosion" as electronic information spreads swiftly, but there's a painful shortage of wisdom. People don't seem to know how to use the information they receive. God's people can pray for wisdom (James 1:5) and find wisdom in the Scriptures. "The fear of the LORD is the beginning of wisdom" (Prov. 9:10).

He is the God of glory (Acts 7:2). Before Abraham and Sarah trusted the true and living God, they worshiped the moon goddess in Ur of the Chaldeans. There is no glory in dead idols and they knew the difference. Jesus temporarily laid aside his glory when he came to earth as a human, but he reclaimed it when he returned to heaven and has shared that glory with his own people (John 17:22). Some of that glory radiated from Stephen's face as he addressed the Jewish council (Acts 6:15). "He who glories, let him glory in the LORD" (1 Cor. 1:31).

He is the living God (1 Thess. 1:9). Unlike dead idols made by human hands, the God we worship and serve is living and cannot die. Our God can walk with us, speak to us, help us solve our problems, and fight our battles, and he never wearies of caring for his children. The Holy Spirit is the Spirit of the living God (2 Cor. 3:3) and God's people are "the church of the living God" (1 Tim. 3:15). If we truly know God through faith in Jesus Christ, his life must shine through us in our daily walk, our worship, and our service.

He is the God of peace (Phil. 4:9). God has not declared war on mankind; it is mankind that has declared war on God (Rom. 1:18). Our Lord's first words to the apostles after his resurrection were "Peace be with you" (John 20:19, 21).

He is the God of hope (Rom. 15:13). Those without Christ are without hope; those trusting in Christ have a living hope (1 Pet. 1:3). One day, we shall go to heaven and see Jesus!

We could go on, but this should be enough to thrill the heart of every true Christian with the greatness of God. And he has made a covenant with us!

> For this is God,
> Our God forever and ever;
> He will be our guide
> Even to death.
>
> Psalm 48:14

73

> *So I bought the field* from Hanamel, the son of
> my uncle who was in Anathoth, and weighed out
> to him the money—seventeen shekels of silver.

JEREMIAH 32:9

I suspect that many people thought Jeremiah was very foolish to buy a field that was three miles from Jerusalem and occupied by the besieging Babylonian army. But Jeremiah knew why he bought it: God told him to. It was a sermon in action. The prophet had announced that the Jewish captives in Babylon would return to Judah in seventy years (25:11–12; 29:10; 32:15, 37–44), and now Jeremiah was backing up his words with deeds. Faith without works is dead (James 2:17). That clay vessel containing the property deeds would be a constant reminder of God's promise. Jeremiah would never claim the land, but a member of his family could take the deeds and possess it.

God has used several different means to remind his people of their future blessings and thereby give them confidence in trying times. When Joseph was dying, he assured his brethren they would leave Egypt to go to the land promised to Abraham, Isaac, and Jacob. He commanded them to tell each succeeding generation to take his embalmed body in a coffin and bury it with his ancestors in the Promised Land (Gen. 50:22–26)—and they did (Exod. 13:19; Josh. 24:32; Acts 7:15–16). During the years of bondage in Egypt, that coffin must have given the suffering Jewish people hope. When we visit the burial place of a believer, we usually look down in sadness at the gravestone, but we should look up in joy to the Lord and say, "When you return, you will empty this grave! Hallelujah!"

A coffin encouraged the enslaved Jews in Egypt and a clay jar encouraged the exiled Jews in Babylon, but the Lord has given his people today a simple meal to encourage us to watch for the coming of the Lord (Matt. 26:26–30). At our Lord's last Passover feast with his disciples, Jesus instituted the Lord's Supper and told his disciples to observe it in remembrance of him and in anticipation of his promised return (1 Cor. 11:23–26). Believers participate in this family meal and look back at the cross, look within at their own hearts, and look ahead to the coming of Jesus. "And everyone who has this hope in Him purifies himself, just as He is pure" (1 John 3:3). The church today uses different schedules for observing the Lord's Supper, but it's likely that the early Christians observed it each Lord's Day when they assembled and frequently at the close of an ordinary meal during the week.

The body of each Christian believer is likened to a clay vessel in which the Holy Spirit dwells (2 Cor. 4:7). Why is he there? He has many ministries, but according to Ephesians "the Holy Spirit of promise" has sealed us so that we know we belong to the Lord, that he will one day come for us and take us to our heavenly inheritance (Eph. 1:13–14). The Spirit of God abides with us forever (John 14:16), which means we should have confidence and courage, no matter how difficult life may become. The Spirit of promise focuses our eyes of faith on the promises of God, especially the promise of Christ's return, and assures us that Jesus will keep his promises. So keep looking up! Don't be discouraged and don't plan to quit.

> Then the word of the LORD came to Jeremiah, saying, "Behold, I am the LORD, the God of all flesh. Is there anything too hard for Me?"
>
> Jeremiah 32:26–27

74

Then Jeremiah took another scroll and gave it to Baruch the scribe, the son of Neriah, who wrote on it at the instruction of Jeremiah all the words of the book which Jehoiakim king of Judah had burned in the fire. And besides, there were added to them many similar words.

JEREMIAH 36:32

A new generation. Jehoiakim, son of Josiah, was on the throne of Judah. His father was a great man of faith and courage, but not Jehoiakim. He would not listen to the counsel of the prophet Jeremiah but "did evil in the sight of the LORD" (2 Kings 23:37). Instead of sacrificing personal gain so he could care for his needy people, Jehoiakim built himself a large, expensive palace at a time when Judah needed a better example of leadership (Jer. 22:13–19). During Josiah's reign, the book of the law was found in the temple, and when it was read to Josiah, he tore his clothes, confessed sin, and called the nation to repent (2 Kings 22). But when his son Jehoiakim heard the Scriptures read, he cut the scroll into pieces and burned it! How sad it is when a new generation abandons the faith of their fathers. If Jehoiakim had followed the example of his father, he would have escaped defeat and a disgraceful death.

An ancient temptation. A very old lie controlled the mind and heart of Jehoiakim, a lie first spoken by the devil in the Garden of Eden: "Has God indeed said . . . ?" (Gen. 3:1). "Can you really trust what God says?" The king did not believe that the words of the prophet were God's words or that they had any personal message for him. Some of the king's officers heard the scroll read *and trembled in fear*, but the king paid no attention. He burned the scroll in the fire. Human hands may destroy copies of God's Word, but they can never destroy the Word of God itself. "Forever, O LORD, Your word is settled in heaven" (Ps. 119:89). Jesus said, "Heaven and earth will pass away, but My words will by no means pass away" (Matt. 24:35). Jehoiakim trusted the lies of his advisors and the false prophets, but he would not trust the truth of God from a true prophet. World leaders have made this mistake very often, but "the word of God . . . abides forever" (1 Pet. 1:23).

A gracious restoration. When his scribe Baruch reported to Jeremiah that the king had destroyed the scroll, the prophet "took another scroll" and dictated a duplicate copy. As far as the nation was concerned, this was a gracious act on the Lord's part, but as for the king, it sealed his doom. Destroying the evidence doesn't liberate the criminal! The record stands that Jehoiakim rejected God's will and paid dearly for his folly, and we today have the record in Scripture and can learn from it. The lost world hates the Scriptures because they shed light on the wickedness of the human heart. At the same time the Scriptures reveal the gracious heart of a loving God. "For everyone practicing evil hates the light and does not come to the light, lest his deeds should be exposed" (John 3:20).

A privileged obligation. Those in authority may ignore the Scriptures and even want to destroy them, but God's people have the privileged obligation to love God's Word, read and study it, and then obey it. We should welcome it "not as the word of men, but as it is in truth, the word of God, which also effectively works in you who believe" (1 Thess. 2:13). It isn't enough just to believe the Bible; we must receive it into our very being as we do our food and drink. Are we taking advantage of this privilege?

> Man shall not live by bread alone, but by every word that proceeds from the mouth of God.
>
> Matthew 4:4

75

> Then they sent someone to take Jeremiah from
> the court of the prison, and committed him to
> Gedaliah . . . that he should take him home. So
> *he dwelt among the people.*
>
> JEREMIAH 39:14

Early in his ministry, Jeremiah wanted to find a lodging place in the wilderness where he could get away from the people and not have to witness their godless activities (Jer. 9:1–6). But let's not be too hard on him, because Moses became so distressed with the Israelites that he wanted to die (Num. 11:10–15), and David prayed for wings that he might fly away from Jerusalem and have some peace (Ps. 55:6–8). By the grace of God, all three stayed on the job and served the Lord and his people. The Babylonian captain offered to take Jeremiah to Babylon where he would be cared for, but he chose to live with his people. When you feel like running away, consider the factors that kept Jeremiah going when the going was tough.

He was in close communion with God. "Do not be afraid of their faces," the Lord told Jeremiah when he called him, "for I am with you to deliver you" (Jer. 1:8; *see* vv. 17–19). Jeremiah believed God's promises and the Lord did not fail him. The king of Judah and his officers failed the people and tried to flee the city, but they were caught and judged (39:1–10). They ran away because they were hirelings and not shepherds (John 10:12–13). Jeremiah wept over his people and wished he could weep even more (Jer. 4:19; 9:1; 23:9). He was a true patriot who loved his nation and tried desperately to save it from ruin, and that love came from his close walk with God, for the Lord loves Israel with an everlasting love (31:3). The word *heart* is used seventy-five times in Jeremiah and Lamentations.

He accepted his calling. Jeremiah knew his work would not be easy. He would have to root things out and tear things down before he could plant and build (1:9–10). The godless leaders would oppose him, but the Lord would make him a fortified city, an iron pillar, and bronze walls (1:17–19). The only way to go forward is to take your stand. God made him an assayer to turn up the heat and separate the gold from the dross (6:27–30), and the people did not want that. The false prophets were deceitful doctors who lied about the nation's condition and gave medicine that did no good (6:13–14; 8:21–22). Jeremiah was like a lamb led to the slaughter (11:19) and a shepherd trying to lead a rebellious flock (13:17; 23:1–6). He had to wear the yoke (chaps. 27–28), *but the Lord was yoked with him and helped him carry the load.* We can claim the same privilege as we serve the Lord (Matt. 11:28–30). Jeremiah is known as "the weeping prophet" (Jer. 9:1; 13:17; 14:17), but Jesus wept during his ministry (Luke 19:41; John 11:35) and so did Paul (Acts 20:19).

He cared for God's people. He lived with them, prayed for them, and shared God's promises with them when he could have been living comfortably in Babylon. *He always told them the truth.* Had the leaders accepted God's Word, the city and the people would have been delivered from destruction. Like David and Jesus, Jeremiah saw them as sheep without a shepherd and loved them though they misunderstood him and rejected his message (2 Sam. 24:17; Matt. 9:36; *see* 2 Cor. 2:15). "Love never fails" (1 Cor. 13:8) even if it seems we have failed miserably, because love makes us more like Jesus; and Jesus also dwelt among the people and sought to help them.

I have compassion for these people; they have already been with me three days and have nothing to eat.

Mark 8:2 TNIV

76

And *do you seek great things* for yourself? Do
not seek them; for behold, I will bring adversity
on all flesh. . . . . But I will give your life to you as
a prize in all places, wherever you go.

JEREMIAH 45:5

The events in this short chapter probably occurred
between verses 8 and 9 of chapter 36. The scribe
Baruch had written the "judgment scroll" and read
it to the high officials and then to King Jehoiakim, who had
destroyed it. Baruch had then written a duplicate scroll with
additions at Jeremiah's dictation. All this hard work, plus the
actions and attitudes of the king, had disturbed Baruch and
he had become discouraged. But the Lord spoke to Jeremiah,
who spoke to Baruch, and the problem was solved. When you
find yourself in a similar situation, call these facts to mind.

God knows how you feel. The name Baruch means "blessed
of the Lord," but after all he had been through, he didn't feel
especially blessed. According to chapter 36, Baruch had read
the scroll to the people in the temple and then to the king's
officers in the palace. When the king had heard the scroll
read, he cut it to pieces and burned it, and then tried to have
Baruch arrested, but God hid him. And after all this, Baruch
had to write the scroll again, so it's no wonder he was sigh-
ing, fainting, and finding no rest! We don't get tired of the
Lord's work, but we can become weary *in* the Lord's work.
He was ready to say to Jeremiah what Peter asked Jesus: "See,
we have left all and followed You. Therefore what shall we
have?" (Matt. 19:27). Satan was whispering in Baruch's ear,
"What will you get out of it? *I* have a better deal for you!"
The Lord knew all about it and had a better solution.

God knows what we desire. The heart of every problem
is the problem in the heart. Baruch had a serious problem in

his heart and the Lord knew what it was: Baruch was seeking greater things than he was receiving from Jeremiah. Baruch came from a highly esteemed family in Judah. His grandfather Maaseiah had been governor of Jerusalem under King Josiah (2 Chron. 34:8), and his brother Seraiah was a member of King Jehoiakim's staff (Jer. 32:12; 36:4; 51:59). With these kinds of "connections," Baruch probably could have gotten a palace appointment and escaped persecution. *But the safest place in the world is in the will of God.* Baruch probably thought that the leaders would accept God's warning and repent, and then he would be in good standing with the people and the king's court. Perhaps there would be a revival as there was in Josiah's day and God would rescue the nation. Baruch's hopes were in vain, but God knew all about them and assured Baruch that his life was not in danger.

God wills what is best. We don't need "great and mighty things" for ourselves; our task is to ask God to do "great and mighty things" so that he will be exalted (Jer. 33:3). If, like Mary, we surrender all to him, we will one day be able to say as she did, "For He who is mighty has done great things for me" (Luke 1:49). It did not make God happy to bring destruction and captivity to Judah, Jerusalem, and the people, but it had to be done. The Lord had given them their land and blessed them in it, but their sins had violated the covenant and he had to discipline them (Jer. 45:4). Furthermore, Jeremiah paid a greater price in serving than Baruch did, for he was lied about, imprisoned, and beaten. He often felt the sorrows of the people who were about to be taken captive and wept over them. His reward? He was so godly that the people thought Jesus was Jeremiah (Matt. 16:14)! What a compliment to Jeremiah!

> Be of the same mind toward one another. Do not set your mind on high things, but associate with the humble. Do not be wise in your own opinion.
>
> Romans 12:16

77

Through the LORD's mercies we are not con-
sumed, because His compassions fail not. *They
are new every morning*; great is Your faithfulness.

LAMENTATIONS 3:22–23

On the desk adjacent to my computer I have a small reproduction of Rembrandt's "The Prophet Jeremiah Lamenting the Destruction of Jerusalem." The painting certainly reflects the sorrow expressed in Jeremiah's book of Lamentations. Our text follows eighteen verses of misery and introduces a section on mercy that speaks to us today no matter how difficult life may be.

Each morning, let's rejoice! Our circumstances may change and our feelings about our circumstances may change, *but our Father in heaven never changes!* "I am the LORD, I do not change" (Mal. 3:6). Each sunrise means we are a day older, but the Lord never ages for he is eternal. This means that each of his divine attributes is unchanging and we can depend on him always to be merciful, compassionate, and faithful (Lam. 3:22–23). God in his mercy does not give us what we do deserve, and in his grace and love he gives us what we don't deserve. The Hebrew word translated *mercies* in our text can also be translated "covenant love" and "loving-kindness." From day to day, we have no idea what our family members, teachers, friends, or bosses will be like, but we know what God will be like, so let's rejoice.

Each morning, let's remember. The Jewish people who were lamenting with Jeremiah knew what had happened each morning in Jewish history and at the Jewish temple. They knew that during Israel's wilderness wanderings, each morning the manna fell from heaven to feed the people (Exod. 16); and each morning we need to feed on the Word of God so we have the spiritual strength we need for the tasks of the day. "Man shall not live by bread alone, but by every word that proceeds from the mouth of God" (Matt. 4:4). The priests each morning stirred up the fire on the altar (Lev. 6:12) so the sacrifices could be offered, and Paul used this activity to encourage Timothy to stir up the fire in his heart (2 Tim. 1:6). The priests offered burnt offerings each morning (Exod. 29:38–46), and we should offer ourselves to the Lord each morning (Rom. 12:1–2). The burning of incense each morning (Exod. 30:7) speaks of prayer (Ps. 141:1–2), and we must begin the day with prayer and communion with the Lord. And let's be sure to praise and thank God before we lay our day's burdens before him (1 Chron. 23:30). When I was a seminary student, each summer I had a fulltime job that involved shift-work, so I had to adjust my schedule each week; but it worked out fine because no matter what the hour, I could meet with the Lord.

Each morning, let's receive. In Lamentations 3:22–24, Jeremiah mentions four attributes of God: mercy, compassion, faithfulness, and hope. Mercy speaks of his forgiveness, so let's not carry yesterday's sins into the new day. Compassion speaks of God's provision for each need, so let's ask and receive, "casting all your care upon Him, for He cares for you" (1 Pet. 5:7). Each morning, pray your way through that day's schedule and tell him what you need. The day will go better. God's faithfulness assures us that he is dependable to be with us and to keep his promises. As for hope, we need it, because matters don't always work out as we planned.

Our daily meeting with the Lord is the secret of "newness of life" for each day's demands (Rom. 6:4), so start walking the "new and living way" (Heb. 10:20).

> The LORD is good to those who wait for Him,
> To the soul who seeks Him.
>
> Lamentations 3:25

78

> Then I looked, and *behold, a whirlwind was coming* out of the north, a great cloud with raging fire engulfing itself; and brightness was all around it and radiating out of its midst like the color of amber, out of the midst of the fire.
>
> EZEKIEL 1:4

A new location. Ezekiel the priest was taken to Babylon with the second wave of exiles but, being away from the temple and its furnishings, he could not continue his usual ministry. When the Lord relocates us, we might conclude that our ministry is over, but that may not be true. Joseph had a ministry in an Egyptian jail that led him to his becoming second ruler of the land and saving the Jewish nation. During wartime, many Christians in uniform have found opportunities to serve Christ in foreign lands. No matter where God leads us, he goes before us and prepares the way. God is everywhere and can work through us no matter where we are in his will. If the Lord has led you to a new place and you feel abandoned and alone, be encouraged! He has a job for you to do, so be alert!

A different vocation. God called Ezekiel from being a priest to being a prophet, a much more difficult calling. Jeremiah had the same experience and so did John the Baptist, both of whom had fathers who were priests. A priest's work was primarily routine, for everything he needed to know was written in the first five books of the Old Testament. But there was nothing routine about the life of a prophet. In fact, a prophet might be attacked, jailed, or even executed. A Jewish priest had a certain amount of security, but prophets faced opposition and danger. A priest's ministry was to maintain and protect the past so that each new generation could know

God and fellowship with him. A prophet's task was to challenge the present when kings, priests, and common people disobeyed the Lord and needed to repent. That's why prophets weren't usually popular; but without their faith and courage, there could be no happy future for the nation. The temple ministry involved teamwork among the priests and Levites, but prophets often had to go it alone. Ezekiel at least had a wife to help bear the burdens, but then she died—and Ezekiel preached her funeral! He didn't have an easy life, but he was faithful to the end.

A fearful visitation. God's message came to Ezekiel in the form of a vision of a storm brewing in the northern sky. In the midst of the fiery cloud, he saw a throne on a large crystal platform with wheels full of eyes at each corner of the platform, wheels that could simultaneously turn in any direction. Four living creatures, each with four faces, were under the platform and in charge of its movements. It was a vision of God on his throne and at work in his world to accomplish his purposes. A storm from the north was coming, and that storm would bring judgment to the people and destruction to Jerusalem and the temple. There was also a rainbow around the throne that spoke of God's grace in the midst of the storms of life. God would judge his people, but where sin abounds, his grace also abounds (Rom. 5:20), and in his wrath, the Lord would remember mercy (Gen. 9:8–17; Hab. 3:2).

Each generation in history has experienced storms, and ours will not escape. In each generation false prophets have predicted "peace and safety," but the storms have swept down just the same (1 Thess. 5:3), and judgment begins in the house of the Lord (Ezek. 9:4–6; Jer. 25:29; 1 Pet. 4:17–18). Are we ready?

> Fire and hail, snow and clouds;
> Stormy wind, fulfilling His word.
>
> Psalm 148:8

79

> Like the appearance of a rainbow in a cloud on
> a rainy day, so was the appearance of the bright-
> ness all around it. This was the appearance of the
> likeness of *the glory of the* LORD.
>
> EZEKIEL 1:28

*A*re you surprised to find God's glory in the storm? We associate storms with darkness and destruction, so why would God put his glory there? Everything about God is glorious: his name (Ps. 72:19), his work (111:3), his power (Col. 1:11), his throne (Jer. 17:12), his creation (Ps. 19:1)—and his judgments. He receives glory when he judges sin just as when he answers prayer. In Psalm 29 David describes a storm he had witnessed while in the wilderness, and he uses the word "glory" four times. The people of Judah were far from God and their rulers were not interested in changing their ways, so God sent them "hurricane Nebuchadnezzar" and the Babylonian army devastated Judah and Jerusalem. God is glorified by our obedience (Matt. 5:16), but if we persist in disobeying him, he will get glory in the discipline he sends. The greatest suffering God ever gave to a person was when he laid the world's sins on Jesus (Isa. 53:6), and yet the cross brings great glory to the Lord. "God forbid that I should glory, save in the cross of our Lord Jesus Christ," wrote Paul (Gal. 6:14 KJV). If we trust him, God can get glory from our storms as well as from our peaceful successes.

Are you shocked to see God's glory in the presence of idols? Ezekiel in Babylon knew more about what was happening in Jerusalem than did the people in the city! God let him see the sins of the priests as they worshiped idols *in the temple of the Lord* (Ezek. 8). In hidden places in the temple as well as in the open courtyards, the priests were worshiping idols, from the sun to abominable things creeping on the earth. Idolatry was always one of the major sins of the Hebrew people and God often disciplined them for their disobedience, but for them to worship idols in God's temple was *incredible*! "Professing to be wise, they became fools, and changed the glory of the incorruptible God into an image" (Rom. 1:22–23). God will not share worship with idols. "I am the LORD, that is My name; and My glory I will not give to another, nor My praise to graven images" (Isa. 42:8). The Lord removed his glory from the temple (Ezek. 8:4; 9:3; 10:4, 18; 11:22–23) and then permitted the Babylonian army to destroy the temple.

Are you accustomed to seeing God's glory in the church? God's glory had been in the tabernacle (Exod. 40:34), but the sins of the priests caused it to leave, and the people said "Ichabod—the glory has departed" (1 Sam. 4:19–22). When Solomon dedicated the temple, the glory of God moved in (1 Kings 8:1–11), but now God's glory was abandoning his house and his people. In the person of the Holy Spirit, God's glory dwells in every believer, making our bodies God's temples (1 Cor. 6:19–20). He also dwells in each local church that is true to the Lord (1 Cor. 3:9–17). "Do you not know that you are the temple of God and that the Spirit of God dwells in you?" (1 Cor. 3:16). Note the warning that follows in verse 17: "If anyone destroys God's temple, God will destroy that person; for God's temple is sacred, and you together are that temple" (TNIV). Paul prayed that there might be "glory in the church" (Eph. 3:21) as a result of the Spirit at work in the lives of the dedicated assembly. Otherwise, Jesus may end up outside the church, trying to get in (Rev. 3:14–20). How tragic it is when a local church does everything but glorify Jesus Christ. The glory of God will return to the Jewish temple (Ezek. 43:1–5), and when a local church is prepared, the Spirit will return and bring power and blessing—and Jesus will be glorified.

And the glory of the LORD came into the temple by way of the gate which faces toward the east. The Spirit lifted me up and brought me into the inner court; and behold, the glory of the LORD filled the temple.

Ezekiel 43:4–5

80

When I saw it, *I fell on my face*, and I heard a voice of One speaking.

EZEKIEL 1:28

God called Ezekiel to be his spokesman to the Jewish prisoners of war living in Babylon, while Jeremiah served the people left in Judah. The first step in his "ordination" was for Ezekiel to behold the glorious throne of God in the midst of a storm. The purpose of Christian life and service is to magnify God's glory, no matter what the circumstances might be. Unless we are equipped by the Lord, our labor will be in vain. How did Ezekiel respond?

He fell on his face before the glory of the Lord. In contemporary speech, to "fall on your face" means to "fail miserably and be embarrassed almost beyond apology." But in biblical terms, it means to humble ourselves before the Lord and give everything to him, to be so overwhelmed by his greatness and glory that we see ourselves as nothing. It is to say with John the Baptist, "He must increase, but I must decrease" (John 3:30). Abraham fell prostrate before the Lord (Gen. 17:3, 17), as did Moses and Aaron (Num. 14:5), Daniel (Dan. 8:17), and the apostle John (Rev. 1:17). In the Garden of Gethsemane, Jesus fell on his face and prayed to the Father as he prepared to go to the cross (Matt. 26:36–39). At least six times in his book, Ezekiel records that he fell on his face before the Lord. "Pride goes before destruction, and a haughty spirit before a fall" (Prov. 16:18). "The worst enemy a man has is himself," said D. L. Moody. "His pride and self-confidence often ruin him." "God resists the proud, but gives grace to the humble" (James 4:6).

He stood on his feet in the strength of the Lord (Ezek. 2:1–2). God's commandment carries with it God's enablement.

166

"Then the Spirit entered me when He spoke to me, and set me on my feet" (v. 2). We today can claim the Spirit's power as did Ezekiel. "Humble yourselves in the sight of the Lord, and He will lift you up" (James 4:10). Five times in his book, Ezekiel tells us that the Lord lifted him up and enabled him to do his work. *The same power of the Spirit that lifted up God's glorious throne also lifted up his humble servant* (Ezek. 1:19–21). The final "lifting up" Ezekiel records is when the Spirit lifted him up and carried him into the new temple where God's glory had returned (43:1–5). The prophet began with glory and ended with glory, but that's the way the Christian life should develop—"from glory to glory" (2 Cor. 3:18). Ministry requires believers who will take their stand, regardless of personal weakness or the opposition of the enemy. "'Not by might nor by power, but by My Spirit,' says the LORD of Hosts" (Zech. 4:6).

He set his face in the will of the Lord (Ezek. 3:8–11). Nine times the Lord told Ezekiel to set his face against a "target" and speak the words he gave him (6:2; 13:17; 20:46; 21:2; 25:2; 28:21; 29:2; 35:2; 38:2). This meant courageously delivering God's message in God's power and not wavering or weakening because of the consequences. "Behold, I have made your face strong against their faces" (3:8). He said something similar to Jeremiah: "Do not be afraid of their faces, for I am with you to deliver you" (Jer. 1:8). Like Jesus going to Jerusalem, the prophet set his face steadfastly and obeyed the will of God (Luke 9:51). Ezekiel's messages were not easy to deliver and his listeners were not sympathetic with him, but he did the work God called him to do, and so should we. The words of Jesus to his Father come to mind:

I have glorified You on the earth. I have finished the work which You have given Me to do.

John 17:4

81

> But you, son of man, hear what I say to you. Do
> not be rebellious like that rebellious house; *open
> your mouth and eat* what I give you.

EZEKIEL 2:8

When Ezekiel ate the scroll, he joined an illustrious fellowship of believers who have been spiritually nourished by the Scriptures. The list begins with Job saying, "I have treasured the words of His mouth more than my necessary food" (Job 23:12). Moses told Israel that "man shall not live by bread alone; but man lives by every word that proceeds from the mouth of the LORD" (Deut. 8:3). Jesus quoted these words when he confronted Satan in the wilderness and defeated him (Matt. 4:1–4). "How sweet are Your words to my taste," wrote the psalmist, "sweeter than honey to my mouth" (Ps. 119:103). Jeremiah, Ezekiel's fellow prophet, said, "Your words were found, and I ate them, and Your word was to me the joy and rejoicing of my heart; for I am called by Your name" (Jer. 15:16). The apostle John also ate a scroll (Rev. 10:8–11), and it was sweet as honey in his mouth but bitter in his stomach.

Reading and hearing the Scriptures should be as pleasant an experience to us as consuming a sumptuous banquet. After all, receiving the Word of God into our hearts (Ezek. 3:10) is not punishment but nourishment and enjoyment. One of the first symptoms of decline in our spiritual walk is our loss of appetite for the Scriptures. Eating is a familiar metaphor for learning. People say to a high-powered salesperson or politician, "I can't swallow that," or "I'll have to chew on that for a while." We say to the preacher, "You gave me food for thought," or maybe we say, "That young preacher has too many half-baked ideas." A friend said to me, "I really devoured that book." Receiving spiritual truth is like eating food, and the truth goes into our mind and heart and gradually transforms our inner person.

Each believer must set aside time daily to read the Bible, meditate on it, digest it, and let it produce spiritual growth. Too many busy Christians swallow "religious junk food" that actually makes them weaker and not stronger. We should come away from our daily quiet time with the taste of honey on our tongue and the warmth of God's love in our hearts (Luke 24:32), and we should meditate on these blessings during the day. The inspired author of Psalm 119 met the Lord in the morning (v. 147) and with the Spirit's help carried the experience with him all day (vv. 97, 164). In fact, even at night he communed with the Lord in the Word (vv. 55, 62). Many times the Lord has awakened me during the night and taught me truths I never saw while reading my Bible at my desk. God's "night school" is worth attending.

Jesus is the perfect example of what it means to live by the Word of God. When he was twelve years old, he tarried at the temple and discussed the Scriptures with the Jewish teachers (Luke 2:41–50). During his ministry, he could effectively quote the Scriptures to instruct seekers and refute his opponents. The secret? He listened to his Father daily. "The Lord GOD has given Me the tongue of the learned, that I should know how to speak a word in season to him who is weary. He awakens Me morning by morning. He awakens My ear to hear as the learned" (Isa. 50:4). Do your ears wake up each morning to hear the Lord speak? Are the Lord's testimonies bringing joy to your heart each day? Open your eyes to the Word of God and hear what the Lord has to say.

> Your testimonies I have taken as a heritage forever,
> For they are the rejoicing of my heart.
>
> Psalm 119:111

82

So I said, "Ah, Lord God! Indeed *I have never
defiled myself* from my youth till now; I have never
eaten what died of itself or was torn by beasts, nor
has abominable flesh ever come into my mouth."

EZEKIEL 4:14

God *prepares his servants.* As I look back on more than
six decades of ministry, I can see more clearly how the
Lord has prepared me for my work and prepared my
work for me. Ezekiel's preparation is recorded in the first three
chapters of his book. First, God revealed his throne of glory and
some of the intricate workings of his providence. Our motive
in ministry is to glorify the Lord, and the method of ministry
is to submit to his will. He knows what he is doing. We "reign
in life" only when Christ reigns in our lives (Rom. 5:17). But
God also revealed the impending storm that announced the
judgment of Jerusalem. He commanded Ezekiel to be a faithful watchman and warn people of the wrath to come (Ezek.
4:16–21). The Spirit of God then took control of the prophet
(2:1–2) and he was commanded to eat the Word of God and let
it become a part of his very being. He was to proclaim God's
Word in the power of the Spirit (3:4–15) and the Lord would
do the rest. The Scriptures and the Spirit must always work
together, and the servant must always submit to the Savior.

God instructs his servants. When his ministry began in
chapter 4, Ezekiel was told exactly what to do: he was to
"play war" before the people! What a childish thing to ask
a dignified priest to do! There are several of these unusual
ministry events in the book; I call them "action sermons."
The exiles in Babylon were so blind to God and his ways
that the prophet had to treat them like children and demonstrate the truth as well as declare it. He "played" war

and also "played" barber (chap. 5). His most costly "action sermon" was when his wife died and he was not allowed to mourn (24:15–27). These "action sermons" remind us that the life of a witness is an important part of the message of the witness. No matter how strange God's instructions may seem, we must accept them and obey them, for "the foolishness of God is wiser than men" (1 Cor. 1:25).

God tests his servants. When God commanded Ezekiel to cook his "soldier's rations" over human waste, he was testing him. Remember, Ezekiel was a priest, and the priests had to remain ceremonially clean or they could not serve. They had to know the difference between "clean" and "unclean" and teach that difference to the people (Ezek. 44:23; Lev. 10:10). If the Israelites failed to maintain this standard, they would be cast out of their land (Lev. 18:24–30). In fact, they had already been cast out because they had rejected the holy and chosen the unholy. Being a priest, Ezekiel had obeyed God's laws against ritual defilement, even to the extent of using only cow's dung as fuel when cooking his meals. "He who is faithful in what is least is faithful also in much" (Luke 16:10). Christians today need not be concerned about foods because "there is nothing unclean of itself" (Rom. 14:14) and we are not defiled by what goes into our mouth but by what comes out (Matt. 15:11; Mark 7:18–23). Our abuse of this freedom may not hurt us, but it might cause a weaker brother or sister to stumble (Rom. 14). Had Ezekiel used human waste as fuel, the people would have known it and the prophet would have injured his reputation and his opportunity to minister to the people. His "action sermons" would have meant nothing. The law of love dictates that we think of others and not just of ourselves.

Therefore let us pursue the things which make for peace and the things by which one may edify another. Do not destroy the work of God for the sake of food.

Romans 14:19–20

83

> "Utterly slay old and young men, maidens and little children and women; but do not come near anyone on whom is the mark; *and begin at my sanctuary.*" So they began with the elders who were before the temple.
>
> EZEKIEL 9:6

The Lord gave orders to six men (angels?) assigned to slay the people in Jerusalem who were worshiping idols. A seventh man was to go before them and put a mark on the foreheads of the godly remnant who would be spared, but the rest would be slain. If we had been there, how would the Lord have classified us?

Are we disobedient leaders who lead others astray? King Manasseh had moved idolatry into the temple, and the Lord had announced that judgment would ultimately come to Jerusalem if the people did not repent and return to him (2 Kings 21). Since their years in Egypt, the Israelites had a weakness for worshiping idols. Ezekiel 8 records how godless the priests and people were as they worshiped the sun, creeping things, and abominable beasts. The king, the princes, and the false prophets supported this new religion that offended the God of Abraham, Isaac, and Jacob. We must lead God's people to worship God according to his Word and enabled by the Holy Spirit.

Are we feeble followers who go with the crowd? "You shall not follow a crowd to do evil," Moses warned the people at Sinai (Exod. 23:2). He should see today's "crowd culture"! While Moses was on the mountain with the Lord, his brother Aaron was following the crowd and manufacturing a god for them to worship in Moses's absence (Exod. 32). When Moses rebuked his brother, Aaron blamed the people. At Kadesh Barnea, the gateway to Canaan, the crowd refused to believe God and listen to Caleb and Joshua, and for this sin, the nation wandered in the wilderness for thirty-eight years and the old generation died off. King Saul had no fear of the Lord but instead listened to the voice of the people (1 Sam. 15:24). He was more concerned with being popular with the people than pleasing the Lord. Are we walking on the difficult, narrow way that leads to life or the popular, broad way that leads to death (Matt. 7:13–14)?

Are we heartbroken mourners who weep over the state of the church? The Lord instructed the man with the inkhorn to put a mark on the forehead of every person who sighed and cried over the sins being committed in the Lord's temple, and they would escape the judgment (Ezek. 9:4–5). How easy it is to become complacent about bad situations, but if we truly love Christ, we weep and pray and cry out to God to send revival. Ezekiel was one of the burdened mourners (6:11–14), following the example of King Josiah (2 Kings 22:13–20), Ezra (Ezra 9), Jeremiah (Jer. 13:15–17), and Daniel (Dan. 9). Jesus wept over Jerusalem (Luke 19:41–42) and Paul wept over worldly professed Christians in the churches (Phil. 3:17–19; 2 Cor. 12:21). "Rivers of water run down from my eyes, because men do not keep Your law" (Ps. 119:136).

Are we in danger of death? How we treat the church of the living God determines how he will treat us (1 Cor. 3:17). God killed Nadab and Abihu (Lev. 10) for defiling the tabernacle, and Ananias and Sapphira for lying to the church (Acts 5:1–11). People were becoming sick and were dying in the Corinthian church because they were abusing the Lord's Supper (1 Cor. 11:27–34). It's a solemn thought that God's judgment begins in the house of God. We have been given much, and much shall be required of us (Luke 12:48).

> For the time has come for judgment to begin at the house of God; and if it begins with us first, what will be the end of those who do not obey the gospel of God?
>
> 1 Peter 4:17

84

> Son of man, these men have set up *their idols
> in their hearts*, and put before them that which
> causes them to stumble into iniquity. Should I let
> Myself be inquired of at all by them?

Ezekiel had a wife and lived in his own house, thus obeying the instructions Jeremiah had given the exiles in the letter he sent them (Jer. 29:5–6). The elders of the Jewish people visited the prophet in his house, outwardly seeming concerned but inwardly worshiping idols. Ezekiel was a man with *a devoted heart*, wholly yielded to the Lord. Like Daniel, he "purposed in his heart that he would not defile himself" by living as the Babylonians lived (Dan. 1:8). God gave Ezekiel messages for the people, but the people were not prepared to hear and obey. They, too, had idols in their hearts. "The secret of the LORD is with those who fear Him, and He will show them His covenant" (Ps. 25:14). God's servants know what is going on. Moses knew God's ways but the people knew only his acts (Ps. 103:7). The servants at the wedding feast in Cana knew where the wine came from (John 2:9) and the nobleman's servants knew when the boy started healing (John 4:51–52). "I have called you friends," Jesus said, "for all things that I heard from My Father I have made known to you" (John 15:15).

The Jewish elders seated before Ezekiel were men with *divided hearts*, and the Lord told his prophet he was not sure they deserved to hear any word from him (Ezek. 14:3). These men pretended to obey the Law of Moses, but their hearts belonged to the idols and they were breaking the first two commandments (Exod. 20:1–6). It was because of their idolatry that the Jewish people were now exiles in Babylon while Jerusalem and the temple were being attacked. Someone has said that "a change in circumstances does not overcome a flaw in character." God deported the Jews to Babylon and they brought their evil hearts with them! Divided hearts are dangerous, for "a double-minded man [is] unstable in all his ways" (James 1:8). I read about a man who took an unchurched friend to a Quaker meeting where the worshipers sit in silence until the Spirit leads one of them to speak, but that day nobody spoke. As they left, the man apologized to his friend for what seemed to be a wasted hour, but the man said, "Oh, no! Don't apologize! Sitting in that silence, I thought up more ways to make money than I would have done in my office!"

The Lord is *a discerner of our hearts* and "searches all hearts and understands all the intent of the thoughts" (1 Chron. 28:9). If what is in our hearts as we sit in church were flashed on the screen, would we be embarrassed? What idols are in our hearts? Sports heroes? Television and movie celebrities? Money? Cars? Houses? Business achievements? Recognition? Worldly pleasures? Good looks? Praise? "Seek first the kingdom of God and His righteousness," said Jesus, "and all these things shall be added to you" (Matt. 6:33). The so-called good things of life are only "fringe benefits" when we put Jesus first in our lives. It only leads to tragedy when we start worshiping and serving "the creature rather than the Creator" (Rom. 1:25).

"Keep your heart with all diligence, for out of it spring the issues of life" (Prov. 4:23). We received new hearts when we trusted Jesus and gave ourselves to him (Ezek. 11:19; 18:31; 36:26), so why should we defile ourselves with old sins? When Jesus Christ is enthroned in our hearts, those old idols have to go (1 Pet. 3:15)!

> My son, give me your heart,
> And let your eyes observe my ways.
>
> Proverbs 23:26

175

85

> So *I sought for a man* among them who would
> make a wall, and stand in the gap before Me on
> behalf of the land, that I should not destroy it;
> but I found no one.

EZEKIEL 22:30

Isaiah, Jeremiah, and Ezekiel had all told the kingdom of Judah that the Lord was sending judgment because of the nation's idolatry. The leaders of the nation, the priests, and the false prophets were all to blame for this plague, but the common people were happy to follow them (Ezek. 22:23–29). There was a godly remnant that was true to the Lord, but they needed someone to step out and take the lead. Is the situation much different today? We don't seem to have an abundance of mature leaders, both men and women, who can make a difference in nations, cities, and churches, people who can turn lethargy into action and defeat into victory. Perhaps you are the one God is seeking! If so, here are some important instructions.

Watch and pray. Ezekiel was commissioned to be a watchman (3:17) and to choose others to keep watch with him (33:1–11). Each of us needs to watch and pray (Neh. 4:9; Mark 14:38) and stay alert, not only for the return of the Lord but also for the coming of Satan and his agents who want to "secretly bring in destructive heresies" that defile the church (2 Pet. 2:1).

Paul warned the Ephesian elders to watch out for the savage wolves that wanted to ravage the flock (Acts 20:28–31), and we heed his warning today. Paul did not suggest that the churches in Ephesus hang out signs saying "Everybody Welcome"—because deceptive, false teachers are not welcome.

Take your stand. The picture in our text is that of a soldier guarding the wall of the city as the enemy attacks. He sees that a part of the city wall is weakening and about to fall, so he takes his stand at the breach *and he becomes the wall.* He becomes a "gap man" who keeps out the enemy. Yes, one person can make a difference. Many times Moses, David, and Paul stood in the gap, and so did Deborah (Judg. 4–5), Hannah (1 Sam. 1–2), and Mary, mother of Jesus (Luke 1:26–56). In Ephesians 6, Paul not only describes the armor of the Christian soldier but also the posture: we are to *stand* and *withstand* (vv. 11, 13, 14). "Gap people" are to be the wall!

Trust the Lord. "This is the victory that has overcome the world—our faith" (1 John 5:4). Not faith in ourselves—our training, experience, self-confidence—but faith in the Lord and his promises. "For the weapons of our warfare are not carnal but mighty in God for pulling down strongholds, casting down arguments and every high thing that exalts itself against the knowledge of God" (2 Cor. 10:4–5). We must fix our eyes of faith on Jesus (Heb. 12:1–2). Compared to David, Goliath was taller, stronger, more experienced, and armed with superior weapons, *but David had faith in the Lord and defeated the giant* (1 Sam. 17).

See it through. "Watch, stand fast in the faith, be brave, be strong" (1 Cor. 16:13). It may be that "he who fights and runs away lives to fight another day," but it is also true that he never becomes a champion and drives the enemy away. "I have fought the good fight," Paul wrote (2 Tim. 4:7) and added the sad news that many of the believers had given up and deserted him (vv. 9–16). How important it is that we end well and can say with Paul, "I have finished the race, I have kept the faith" (v. 7). Jesus Christ is the Commander of the army of the Lord (Josh. 5:13–15) and he is looking for "gap people" to make up the wall and defeat the enemy.

Care to volunteer?

> I looked, but there was no one to help,
> And I wondered
> That there was no one to uphold.
>
> Isaiah 63:5

86

The satraps, administrators, governors, and the king's counselors gathered together, and they saw these men on whose bodies *the fire had no power*; the hair of their head was not singed nor were their garments affected, and the smell of fire was not on them.

DANIEL 3:27

The world wants us to conform. Spiritually speaking, this slice of ancient history describes a world very much like our society today, a world that wants believers to conform. We, too, live in a world with powerful leaders who want to be treated like gods and who become angry when they cannot have their own way. These leaders know the value of big crowds and that most people sheepishly play "follow the leader." These celebrities also know the seductive power of music and the controlling power of fear that molds the blind obedience of the masses. Ever since Daniel and his three friends arrived in Babylon, they were under pressure to conform. They were given new names, introduced to new gods, expected to eat new diets, and commanded to obey a new lord—Nebuchadnezzar. If they refused, they would be thrown into a super-hot furnace and destroyed. But as believers, we must obey Romans 12:1–2 and not conform to this world but be transformed by the inward renewal of the Spirit. "Do not love the world or the things in the world," commands the apostle John (1 John 2:15), and James wrote, "Do you not know that friendship with the world is enmity with God?" (James 4:4). Our Lord makes it clear that we "are not of the world" (John 17:14). To conform to the world is to abandon the will of God.

The devil wants us to compromise. These three Hebrew men were not just common citizens but officers in the kingdom

(Dan. 3:12), and Satan surely reminded them of that. They had a responsibility to their leader to be good examples. After all, they were prisoners of war and subject to stern discipline. They could easily compromise by bowing their knees but not their hearts, and who would know the difference? *God would!* Perhaps they could drop something to the ground and bow down to pick it up. Or they could pretend to be sick and stay home. *But faith is living without scheming!* Why adopt the devil's tactics? If we are wearing the belt of truth (Eph. 6:14), then we must walk in the truth (3 John 3–4). Compromise is a lie that takes longer to expose, but once exposed, it does incredible damage and it doesn't help build our character or glorify God. Compromise is the crooked sword of the coward.

The Lord wants us to conquer. "In the world you will have tribulation," Jesus said, "but be of good cheer, I have overcome the world" (John 16:33). He has also defeated the devil (Col. 1:13). Because of their courageous faith, the men's fears were dissolved and the Lord joined them in the fiery furnace! "Fear not, for I have redeemed you; I have called you by your name; you are Mine. . . . When you walk through the fire, you shall not be burned, nor shall the flame scorch you" (Isa. 43:1–2). The fire didn't even make their clothes smell! (God is good at handling details.) God didn't put out the fire; he let it burn but not do any damage. These three men are mentioned in Hebrews 11:32–35 along with other heroes of faith.

Peter reminds us that God's people still face "fiery trials" but that the Lord can see us through (1 Pet. 4:12–19). Let's obey his will, trust him, and allow the Holy Spirit to have his way with our lives. It will be worth it all when we see Jesus.

Yet in all these things we are more than conquerors through Him who loved us.

Romans 8:37

87

My people ask counsel from their wooden idols,
and their staff informs them. For the spirit of
harlotry has caused them to stray, and *they have
played the harlot* against their God.

I n the eyes of God, idolatry is the moral equivalent of
adultery and prostitution, just as anger is the moral
equivalent of murder (Matt. 5:21–30). God made us in
his own image so that we might know him, love him, and
serve him, and therefore become more like him. But very
early in human history, people began to make gods in their
own image and worship idols that could not see them, hear
them, or help them. Today, an idol might be a beautiful au-
tomobile or house, a job, money, fame, an organization we
belong to, or even a theory we believe. Idols can influence
us far more than people realize, and this is so subtle that
people hardly recognize this influence.

In Hosea's day, idolatry was rampant among the Jewish
people. When the kingdom was divided during the reign of
Rehoboam, the southern kingdom of Judah had the temple
and the priesthood and could continue to worship; but Jer-
oboam, ruler of the northern kingdom, did not want his
people going to Judah to worship lest they not return home.
So he set up two golden calves for them to worship, one at
Dan and the other at Bethel, and commanded the people to
worship them (1 Kings 12:21–33). This violated the first two
commandments of the law (Exod. 20:1–6). God had made a
"marriage covenant" with Israel at Sinai and the nation had
pledged their obedience to him (Jer. 2:1–3; 3:1–14; Hos. 2;
Isa. 54:5). When the people went after idols, they were committing adultery and "playing the harlot."

The church as a bride is a familiar metaphor in the New Testament. "Husbands, love your wives, just as Christ also loved the church and gave Himself for her" (Eph. 5:25). Paul wrote to the church at Corinth, "I am jealous for you with godly jealousy. For I have betrothed you to one husband, that I may present you as a chaste virgin to Christ" (2 Cor. 11:2). When a local church in its worship and ministry imitates the world and seeks to please the world, instead of obeying the Scriptures and seeking to please God, it is "playing the harlot" and violating its love relationship with Christ. That was the problem with the church at Ephesus: the people had left their first love. If our motive is numbers we can brag about, or preachers or singers we can extol, or religious entertainment we can enjoy, rather than our love for Jesus, then we are worshiping idols. The crowds may like it, but Jesus will be outside the door trying to get in (Rev. 3:20).

Israel was idolatrous, and some churches are idolatrous, but individual Christians can also be guilty of worshiping substitutes for the Lord. We must be careful not to lose our "honeymoon love" for our Savior (Jer. 2), the love we had in the early days of our walk with Jesus. Then, we took time to read and meditate on the Scriptures and to pray and worship the Lord. Being with God's people in public worship was exciting and enjoyable, but perhaps now it is routine and even boring. At some point we began rushing through our daily devotions, criticizing the worship services, and even looking for excuses not to attend. The idols moved in and crowded out Jesus. The church is "married to Christ," although the public wedding has not yet taken place (Rom. 7:1–4; Rev. 19:6–10), but too often he is ignored. "Love never fails" (1 Cor. 13:8), but we can fail in how we express our love to Jesus.

Therefore, my beloved, flee from idolatry.

1 Corinthians 10:14

181

88

Ephraim has mixed himself among the peoples;
Ephraim is a cake unturned.

HOSEA 7:8

Bread was a basic food of the people in the ancient near east. They usually prepared it on a griddle over a low fire, which meant the cook had to be alert and turn the dough over at just the right time. Otherwise the loaf would be ashes on one side and raw dough on the other. If that happened, the loaf was inedible and had to be thrown away. The prophet Hosea called Ephraim (the northern kingdom) a half-baked people. They were not the Lord's "through and through" but half-baked, worshiping the Lord halfheartedly from hearts devoted to idols. Believers today can commit the same sin by making the same mistakes the people of Ephraim made.

Their first mistake was *not being totally devoted to the Lord.* An Eastern proverb says, "Hypocrites are like bread baked on a griddle—they have two faces." The dough cannot turn itself but needs the cook to do it if the loaf is to be eaten. So the dough has two obligations: (1) to "take the heat" and (2) to yield to the hands of the cook. If it resists the heat or refuses to be turned, it will end up half-baked and totally useless. We don't enjoy the trials of life, but we need them. We like to have our own way and avoid "the heat," but then we are half-baked and useless. The Lord wants us to be tasty loaves of nourishing bread so we can help feed the starving multitudes, and that demands complete surrender to the Lord.

Mistake number two was *compromising with the world.* God commanded the people of Israel not to mingle with the other nations and imitate their godless ways. They were to be "a people dwelling alone, not reckoning itself among the nations" (Num. 23:9). When they conquered the Promised

Land, they were instructed to destroy all the idols and temples dedicated to heathen gods and goddesses. The first two generations of Israelites obeyed, but the third generation began to imitate their neighbors by worshiping idols and committing the gross sins that accompanied the worship, and God had to chasten them (Judg. 2:7–23). "They mingled with the Gentiles and learned their works; they served their idols, which became a snare to them" (Ps. 106:35–36). "Aliens have devoured his strength, but he does not know it" (Hosea 7:9). Satan is so subtle that the backsliding believer too often is ignorant of what is happening.

The third mistake was *not being prepared to serve the Lord*. Israel was to be a light to the Gentiles, pointing them to the true and living God (Isa. 49:6); instead, the darkness of the Gentiles enveloped the Jews and they lived in darkness. The priests, Levites, and prophets taught the people the difference between the clean and the unclean and warned them that God would not tolerate their friendship with the world. God has given the same warning to his people today (1 John 2:15–17; 2 Cor. 6:14–7:1; James 4:1–10). The priests and Levites were devoted to the Lord that they might please God and serve the people. They were not initially "half-baked" but dedicated and prepared to serve, but as the years passed, some of them became "half-baked" and totally unprepared to serve in the sanctuary. God cannot bless and use unprepared workers, and yet there are today preachers, teachers, singers, administrators, mothers, fathers, and other workers who are unfit to serve but by their "service" are weakening the cause of Christ.

We must "take the heat" and yield to the Savior's hands so that we might be willing *and* able servants.

> In a great house there are not only vessels of gold and silver, but also of wood and clay, some for honor and some for dishonor. Therefore if anyone cleanses himself from the latter, he will be a vessel for honor, sanctified and useful for the Master, prepared for every good work.
>
> 2 Timothy 2:20–21

89

> Thus will I do to you, O Israel; because I will do
> this to you, *prepare to meet your God*, O Israel.

Amos opened his book by pronouncing judgment on the Gentile nations for the way they had treated the Jews, and this must have made the kingdoms of Israel and Judah very happy. But then the prophet announced that Israel and Judah would be punished for the sins they had committed against the Lord. God had already disciplined his people by sending drought and famine, blight and mildew, diseases and wars, but now the ultimate judgment would come—death. They would meet not God's "spankings" but God himself! The Assyrian army would invade the northern kingdom of Israel and many of the people would die. If you and I knew that we would die next week, how would we respond? *If we suddenly had to rearrange our lives and alter them dramatically, then there is something wrong with our lives.* We should so live for the Lord that he could call us at any time and we would be prepared. Israel was not prepared for several reasons.

They forgot God's covenant. Before the new generation of Israelites entered the Promised Land, Moses reviewed God's covenant and told them how they were to live (Deut. 27–28). After they were in the land, Joshua reviewed it a second time (Josh. 8:30–35). God told them he would provide for them and protect them as long as they obeyed, but if they disobeyed and became like their neighbors, he would chasten them. The very trials God named in the covenant were what he sent to the land, but the people did not get the message. Instead of worshiping the Lord as he had commanded, they began to worship the dead idols of the other nations, and there was nothing for the Lord to do but to chasten them. "The LORD will judge His people" (Heb. 10:30). Because the believers in the Corinthian church didn't properly observe the Lord's Supper, many of them became weak and sickly and some died (1 Cor. 11:27–32). God means what he says!

They ignored God's calls. The various judgments the Lord sent to the land were "wake-up calls" that the leaders and the people ignored. Five times in Amos 4, the Lord said to them, "you have not returned to Me" (vv. 6–11), but they would not listen. They had given their hearts to the pagan idols and turned their backs on the Lord. Amos begged them to seek God and live (5:4, 6, 14), but they ignored him and died. (Moses gave the same warning in Deuteronomy 30:11–20, and we assume that Joshua also reminded them.) It's been my experience that God always deals with me whenever I disobey him and won't listen. But I'm glad he does, because his chastening hand is proof of his loving heart and evidence that I am truly a child of God (Heb. 12:3–11). God doesn't spank the neighbor's children, which is why lost sinners seem to "get away with things."

They didn't take death seriously. Death is the ultimate judgment God can send, and this includes his own children (1 John 5:16–17). For us to deliberately sin and expect to get away with it is contrary to what the Scriptures teach. God has no pleasure in the death of the wicked (Ezek. 18:23, 32) or when he must take the life of one of his own people. It's sad when professed Christians live as though Jesus never died, the Spirit never came, and judgment will never occur; but Amos cries out, "Prepare to meet your God" (Amos 4:12). Need the Lord say more?

It is appointed for men to die once, but after this the judgment.

Hebrews 9:27

90

But Jonah arose to flee to Tarshish from the presence of the LORD.

JONAH 1:3

What is the book of Jonah about? It's not about fish, for the great fish is mentioned only four times. Jonah is named eighteen times, but the Lord God is mentioned thirty-seven times! The book is about God and how he deals with people who want their own way and therefore refuse to obey his will. Surely Jonah knew that he could not run away from God. "Where can I go from Your Spirit? Or where can I flee from Your presence?" (Ps. 139:7). If we ever attempt to hide from God, the consequence will be painful.

The direction of life will be down. Jonah went *down* to the seaport of Joppa and then went *down* into the ship (Jonah 1:3), and then went *down* into the lowest part of the ship where he went to sleep (v. 5). You would think that the combination of his guilty conscience plus the storm would have kept him awake, but he slept soundly. Often when we disobey God, we enjoy a period of quiet confidence that lulls us into a false peace. This is one of Satan's tricks. But that was not the end. Though the Gentile sailors tried to spare Jonah, he insisted that they throw him into the sea, so he went *down* into the sea where a great fish was awaiting him. The fish swallowed Jonah, who went *down* into its stomach. Down, down, down, down! Jonah had a message from God that would save the lives of nearly a million people in Nineveh, but being a patriotic Jew, Jonah wanted the Ninevites to be killed.

The circumstances of life will be stormy. God called the Jewish people to be a blessing to the world (Gen. 12:1–3), but every time they disobeyed God, they brought trouble instead of blessing. The name Jonah means *dove*, but Jonah brought to the ship anything but peace. One child of God out of the will of God can cause more trouble than a troop of unconverted people. Once Jonah was on his rebellious way, the Lord could no longer speak to him but had to use the storm to get his attention. He also lost his prayer power (Jonah 1:6) and his testimony before the Gentile sailors (vv. 7–9), and by seeking to run away from the Lord, he almost lost his life and endangered the lives of the crew. But once Jonah was off the ship, the storm ceased! I have seen families go from storms to blessed quietness once the sin in the home was confessed and forsaken—and it happens in churches too.

The hope of life will be repentance. Jonah probably hoped for a quick death, but God had other plans. It took Jonah three days to get around to praying and seeking forgiveness, but once he repented, God rescued him and put him back on his feet on dry land. Jonah's prayer is a composite of quotations from the book of Psalms, so the Scriptures he memorized came in handy. When the fish vomited Jonah out on dry land, the people who saw it must have been amazed and alarmed, and the news quickly traveled to Nineveh. When Jonah showed up, they were ready to listen, repented of their sins, and were spared judgment. The Lord gave Jonah another chance, just as he did with Abraham, Jacob, Moses, David, and Peter.

Only a gracious God such as the One we worship can take a stubborn, disobedient servant and use him to bring spiritual awakening to a great city. Jesus used Jonah's experience to picture his own resurrection and to emphasize the importance of hearing the Word of God and repenting (Matt. 12:38–41; 16:4). I trust you are not running from God. If you are, change directions and run *to* him and he will give you a new beginning.

The men of Nineveh will rise up in the judgment with this generation and condemn it, because they repented at the preaching of Jonah; and indeed a greater than Jonah is here.

Matthew 12:41

91

He has shown you, O man, what is good; and what
does the LORD require of you but to do justly, to
love mercy, and to *walk humbly with your God?*

MICAH 6:8

This is a courtroom scene (Micah 6:1–5) and God is judging his people. He asks them to present any evidence that he has ever failed them, but there is none. Then the people ask what they can give the Lord to receive his forgiveness, but no sacrifice will suffice (vv. 6–7). Our text reveals what will please God and what he is seeking in our lives.

We must be right with others. It pleases God when we act justly and love mercy. On first sight, these two seem like oil and water, unable to blend, but thanks to the cross that isn't true. On the cross, Jesus took the punishment we justly deserved for our sins, and now God is able to show mercy to us and not violate his own law. Christ died for us and satisfied the justice demanded by God's law, and he rose from the dead so that he could forgive us by his grace. God is both just and the justifier of those who believe in Jesus. Paul discusses this truth in Romans 3:21–31. Because the Lord has forgiven us, we can forgive others. God in his mercy does not give us what we deserve, but in his grace he gives us what we don't deserve; this opens the way for us to forgive others. It isn't possible for us to have true fellowship with the Lord if we are not in fellowship with others (Matt. 5:21–26).

We must want to make progress spiritually. To walk with the Lord means to grow in grace, to overcome weaknesses and sins, and to depend on his leading and his power. Unless we really want to pay the price of spiritual progress, this text cannot help us. Jesus asked the sick man at the Pool of

Bethesda, "Do you want to be made well?" but his reply was only an excuse (John 5:1–7). In spite of this, Jesus healed him and said, "Rise, take up your bed and walk" (v. 8). New life means a new walk, and a new walk enables us to experience new challenges and grow in the Lord. Are you ready to follow Jesus?

We must agree to meet. If you don't know Jesus personally as Savior and Lord, then the only place you can meet him is at Calvary, where he died for you. If you do know Jesus, then you will meet him each day at the throne of grace (Heb. 4:16). The prophet Amos asked, "Can two walk together, unless they are agreed?" (Amos 3:3). The NASB version of this verse reads, "Do two men walk together unless they have made an appointment?" The Father wants us to make a daily appointment with him when he can speak to us from the Scriptures and we can speak to him in prayer. What a privilege it is to fellowship with the God of the universe!

We must walk in humility. If we walked down the street with a friendly neighbor, nobody would pay much attention to us; but if we walked with the mayor or the governor, that might get some attention. God is the greatest person in the universe and we get to walk with him! He is invisible, of course, but people can see us, and they should be able to see that our behavior is different. But how can we walk "humbly" when our companion is the Lord? By realizing how great he is and how small we are! Why would God deign to walk with me and help me? Who am I that he wants my companionship? Whether it is in the furnace (Dan. 3:25), through the deep waters (Isa. 43:2), or in the dark valley (Ps. 23:4), the Lord will walk with us. Enjoying his presence helps to give us a humble heart, and God gives grace to the humble (1 Pet. 5:5–6).

> Surely He scorns the scornful,
> But gives grace to the humble.
>
> Proverbs 3:34

92

> O LORD, *revive Your work* in the midst of the
> years! In the midst of the years make it known;
> in wrath remember mercy.
>
> ━━━━━━━━━━━━━━ HABAKKUK 3:2

The name Habakkuk means "to wrestle" or "to embrace," and in his book, he does both. In the first chapter he wrestles with the Lord because he cannot understand why a holy God would allow the pagan Babylonians to conquer Judah. God said, "I will work a work in your days which you would not believe, though it were told you" (Hab. 1:5). In chapter 2 Habakkuk gets God's view of the situation, and in chapter 3 he "embraces" the Lord and prays that his work would go on! "Keep your work going" is his prayer. No matter how we serve the Lord, we must never forget that it is *God's* work and not ours. Jesus made it clear that he was doing the Father's work (John 4:32–34) and Paul followed his example (1 Cor. 15:58; 16:10; Phil. 1:6). When we realize that we are doing the Lord's work and not our own, it will bring some encouraging changes into our ministry.

We will move from arguing about God's will to accepting God's will. The prophet Habakkuk was walking by sight in the first chapter, trying in his own power to understand God's plan. Surely the Lord would not allow the godless Babylonians to defeat his chosen people, but he did. He also allowed them to destroy Jerusalem and the temple, places where his chosen people were worshiping idols. Because they were blind, unconverted people, the Babylonians worshiped idols; but the Jews knew the true and living God and so their idolatry was worse. The prophet knew the terms of God's covenant with the people, so he should not have been surprised. Our task is not to explain but to believe and obey. We live on promises, not explanations.

We will stop complaining and start rejoicing (Hab. 3:17–18). Once the prophet submitted himself to the Lord, his whole attitude changed. "'For My thoughts are not your thoughts, nor are your ways My ways,' says the LORD" (Isa. 55:8). Now he was praying, "Your will be done. Keep your work going!" In chapter 3 Habakkuk saw the Lord marching triumphantly through history, and at first he was gripped by fear (v. 16). But when he realized Jehovah was working *for* his people and not against them, he began to worship and celebrate. Habakkuk couldn't rejoice in his circumstances but he could rejoice in the Lord (v. 18).

We will depend on God's strength and not our own (v. 19). "Do not sorrow, for the joy of the LORD is your strength" (Neh. 8:10). It is God's work we are doing and he will provide all that we need, including the strength and wisdom required for each day. We live and work a day at a time, and "as your days, so shall your strength be" (Deut. 33:25). How many times I have looked at a week's schedule and wondered if I could make it—but with God's help, I did! "My grace is sufficient for you, for My strength is made perfect in weakness" (2 Cor. 12:9).

We will move from pleasing ourselves to giving God the glory. When we look ahead, we will say, "The earth will be filled with the knowledge of the glory of the LORD, as the waters cover the sea" (Hab. 2:14). When we look back, we will say, "This was the LORD's doing; it is marvelous in our eyes" (Ps. 118:23). When the Lord's work is done the Lord's way for the Lord's glory, all is well.

For of Him and through Him and to Him are all things, to whom be glory forever. Amen.

Romans 11:36

93

> The Lord your God in your midst, the Mighty One, will save; He will rejoice over you with gladness, He will quiet you with His love, *He will rejoice over you* with singing.
>
> ZEPHANIAH 3:17

We need not fret, for God sees what is coming. The prophet writes about two future "days" that relate to the Jewish people: a *judgment day* when the nations will attack Jerusalem (Zeph. 1:1–3:7), and a *joyful day* when the Lord will rescue his people (3:8–20). "Do not fear," the Lord says to them, for he is with them to deliver them (v. 16). *We can depend on his love, for it will never fail.* "There is no fear in love; but perfect love casts out fear" (1 John 4:18). As the psalmist wrote, "God is our refuge and strength, a very present help in trouble" (Ps. 46:1).

Our God not only saves, but he sings. In our text we see God the Father as a loving parent, holding a troubled child in his lap and singing the child to sleep. Imagine! The Father tenderly holds us and soothes our troubled heart. In Matthew 26:30, we find God the Son singing at the Passover feast before going to the garden to pray and then to Calvary to die. We also find Jesus singing after his resurrection victory (Ps. 22:22; Heb. 2:12). The Holy Spirit sings in and through God's church when we assemble for worship and are yielded to him (Eph. 5:18–21). There are times in the Christian's life when nothing seems to bring peace. Circumstances are pressing, people are too busy to listen, and even our prayers seem ineffective. That's the time to be silent before the Lord and let him sing you into peace. Don't try to explain it, because God's peace "surpasses all understanding" (Phil. 4:7); just enjoy it.

But there is even more. The Lord not only sees what is coming, saves us from judgment, and sings to us, but he rejoices over us. We can make God happy! Parents cherish those times when their children bring great joy to their hearts because of some act of spontaneous obedience and love or because of something very special the children have done just to please them. It isn't enough to simply know God's will and do it; we must also do it to please him. Jonah finally got to Nineveh and delivered God's message, but his attitude was all wrong. He hated the people to whom he was preaching and finally went outside the city and pouted, hoping God would destroy it (Jonah 4). Jesus said, "I always do those things that please Him" (John 8:29). The Father wants us to "walk worthy of the Lord, fully pleasing Him" (Col. 1:10). God told the priests in Malachi's day, "I have no pleasure in you" (Mal. 1:10). Our living should be like our giving, "not grudgingly or of necessity, for God loves a cheerful giver" (2 Cor. 9:7).

"He will be quiet in his love" is another way to translate our text. People who constantly tell us they love us can be as irritating as those who rarely tell us, but where our love is growing deeper, *it is expressed in silence as well as in speech*. When the Lord is not speaking to us or doing things for us, he is still loving us; and the "silent love" can be enjoyed just as much as if not more than spoken words. Babies who cannot speak express love to their parents, and parents can express and tell their love to their children even when they are silent. Call for silence in a worship service and people become nervous. With longtime friends, there is a silence of communion that says more than words, and this includes God's silent love for us.

Is the Father rejoicing over us?

> The LORD takes pleasure in those who fear Him,
> In those who hope in His mercy.
>
> Psalm 147:11

94

And the LORD shall be *King over all the earth.*
In that day it shall be—"The LORD is one," and
His name one.

When I was a lad in Sunday School, I was taught that Jesus was a Prophet when he was here on earth and now he is a Priest in heaven, but when he returns he will reign as King on this earth. But that statement is not quite accurate, because Jesus is reigning as King today. He is a priest after the order of Melchizedek, and Melchizedek was both a king and a priest (Heb. 6:20–7:3). Today, Jesus is seated on the throne in heaven at the Father's right hand (Eph. 1:20; Heb. 1:3; 8:1), and he is King.

The King created us. When our Lord created Adam and Eve, he created royalty, for our first parents were given dominion over creation (Gen. 1:26, 28; Ps. 8:6–8). The tragedy is that they lost that dominion when they disobeyed the Lord, ate of the tree of life, and were cast out of the garden (Gen. 3). In Romans 5:12–21, Paul explains that the consequences of that sin touched every human ever born into the world. Because of Adam's disobedience, sin is reigning in this world (Rom. 5:21), and because sin is reigning, death is reigning (5:14, 17); for "the wages of sin is death" (6:23). The King's creation has been marred by sin and death.

The King came to us. Because of his love and grace, the Lord devised a plan of salvation that would rescue us from sin and death. The Son of God was born in Bethlehem, sent by the Father to be the Savior of the world (1 John 4:14). He was born "King of the Jews" (Matt. 2:1–2), and during his ministry on earth he exercised the dominion Adam had lost. He commanded the fish (Matt. 17:24–27; Luke 5:1–11; John

21:1–14), the birds (Matt. 26:31–34, 74–75), and the animals (Mark 1:12–13; Luke 19:30). He had dominion! But he was rejected by his own people. Pilate, the Roman governor, asked him, "Are you the King of the Jews?" and Jesus replied, "My kingdom is not of this world" (John 18:33, 36). In other words, his kingdom is not a political entity but a worshiping and serving community. Jesus will one day reign as "King over all the earth," but today his kingdom is at work wherever his people obey him and pray, "Your kingdom come. Your will be done on earth as it is in heaven" (Matt. 6:10). The crowd shouted to Pilate, "Crucify him!" And the priests said, "We have no king but Caesar!" (John 19:15). Jesus wore a crown of thorns and was crucified for us with a title above his head: "Jesus of Nazareth, the King of the Jews." But in his death and resurrection, Jesus broke the power of sin and death; now grace is reigning, and those who trust Jesus may today "reign in life" (Rom. 5:17, 21). He has made us "kings and priests" (Rev. 1:5–6) and we are seated with him on the throne (Eph. 2:1–7). We may walk in victory and blessings because we "reign in life" through him (Rom. 5:17).

The King is coming again! Jesus promised to return and take those who have trusted him to their home in heaven to reign with him forever (John 14:1–6; Rev. 22:5). There will be a new heaven and a new earth. Meanwhile, our privilege and responsibility is to "worship the King" (Zech. 14:16–17) and serve him faithfully. Jesus is the King of Kings and Lord of Lords (Rev. 17:14; 19:16), King of heaven and King of all the earth.

The Father "has delivered us from the power of darkness and conveyed us into the kingdom of the Son of His love" (Col. 1:13). We are now in the kingdom! Worship the King!

And God will wipe away every tear from their eyes; there shall be no more death, nor sorrow, nor crying; and there shall be no more pain, for the former things have passed away.

Revelation 21:4

95

"From the rising of the sun, even to its going down, *My name shall be great* among the Gentiles; in every place incense shall be offered to My name, and a pure offering; for My name shall be great among the nations," says the LORD of hosts.

The first step down for any church is taken when it surrenders its high view of God," wrote A. W. Tozer in his excellent book *The Knowledge of the Holy.* For "church" you may also substitute "Christian" or "Sunday school teacher" or "missionary." The prophet Malachi ministered to the Jewish exiles who had returned to their land from Babylon to rebuild Jerusalem and the temple. Unfortunately, the level of their spiritual life was not very high. They could have glorified the name of the Lord before the Gentiles, but instead they chose to argue with the Lord. Believers today have three responsibilities when it comes to the names of God.

We must know God's name. In Bible times, names were indications of character and ability, and the names of God tell us who he is and what he can do. *Jehovah* means "I Am Who I Am" (Exod. 3:13–14). He is the self-existent, eternal God who always was, always is, and always will be. *Jehovah-Sabaoth* is "the LORD of hosts, the LORD of the armies of heaven" (1 Sam. 1:3, 11), while *Jehovah-Rapha* is "the LORD who heals" (Exod. 15:22–27). For the battles in life, we must know *Jehovah-Nissi*, "the LORD our banner" (Exod. 17:8–15), who can give us victory. *Jehovah-Shalom* is "the LORD our peace" (Judg. 6:24), and *Jehovah Ra-ah* is "the LORD our shepherd" (Ps. 23:1). I could go on, but I suggest you pursue this study yourself with the help of a good study Bible. To know God's names is to know him better and be able to call on him for the help we need. "Those who know Your name will put their trust in You; for You, LORD, have not forsaken those who seek You" (Ps. 9:10).

We must honor God's name. The priests in the temple were not honoring God's name but were despising it by performing their ministries carelessly and offering the Lord sacrifices unacceptable to him (Mal. 1:6–10). Malachi used the word "contemptible" to describe their work (1:7, 12; 2:9). God demands that we give him our best and serve him in a way that honors his name (1 Chron. 21:24.) The Lord would rather that someone close the temple doors than allow such cheap sacrifices to be offered on his altar (Mal. 1:10; Lev. 22:20). The priests were not rejoicing in their ministry but were weary of the whole thing (Mal. 1:13). "Serve the LORD with gladness; come before His presence with singing" (Ps. 100:2). We must give glory to his name (Mal. 2:2) and fear his name (1:14; 4:2). There was a godly remnant that did fear the Lord and honor his name (3:16–19), and they were the hope of the nation.

We must spread his name abroad. The Lord wanted his name to be "magnified beyond the border of Israel" (1:5). The prophet saw a day when Jews and Gentiles would be one people of God through faith in Jesus Christ (Eph. 2:11–22). When he died on the cross, Jesus tore the veil of the temple, opening the way to God for all people and breaking down the wall that separated Jews and Gentiles (Eph. 2:14) so that we are "all one in Christ Jesus" (Gal. 3:28). The name of Jesus Christ and his gospel must be shared with the world, for there are no borders that must confine us. "Therefore those who were scattered went everywhere preaching the word" (Acts 8:4). Are we doing our part?

> "For My name shall be great among the nations,"
> Says the LORD of hosts.
>
> Malachi 1:11

96

You have wearied the LORD *with your words.*

Have there ever been people in your life who talked so much that it wore you out to listen to them? Perhaps you had a child or sibling who asked questions from breakfast to bedtime, or a student who never stopped talking about nothing, or a co-worker who felt compelled to tell you all the "inside" office news. When I was in the pastorate, I often had to endure the frequent phone calls of parishioners who thought they had problems and wanted me to know every detail. I realize that listening is an important ministry and that people can often talk their way out of their problems, but time is very precious and talk can be cheap.

But why weary *God* with our words when he already knows what's in our minds and on our hearts? He sees the end from the beginning and isn't impressed with our long speeches. Jesus said that only the heathen "think they will be heard for their many words," and he warned us not to be like them (Matt. 6:7–8). God the Father was wearied by Israel's routine worship, the offerings and prayers that did not come from the hearts of his people (Isa. 29:13). In Malachi's day, after the Jews had left Babylon, returned to their land, and rebuilt the temple, the people were sure God would do some great miracle to impress the Gentiles, but the miracle never came. The people argued with the Lord and, worse yet, the priests were bored with their ministries in the new temple (Mal. 1:12–13). The whole fabric of their religious life was weak and they desperately needed revival. God was weary of listening to their insincere prayers and hymns. Do we have this problem today?

Our Lord Jesus Christ had the same problem with the people in his day *and with his own disciples.* A distraught father brought a demonized son to the nine disciples who had not gone with Jesus to the mount of transfiguration, and the men were unable to drive out the demons (Matt. 17:14–21). When Jesus came down from the mountain and beheld the embarrassing scene, he said, "O faithless and perverse generation, how long shall I be with you? How long shall I bear with you?" (v. 17). Jesus then delivered the boy and gave him to his father. But why had the nine disciples failed? "Because of your unbelief," Jesus told them (v. 20). They were "faithless and perverse," and apparently had not been praying and fasting (v. 21). Jesus had already given them the power to cast out demons (10:1), but in his absence, the nine disciples had grown lax in their spiritual discipline. That is one of the tragic consequences of a weak spiritual life: we cannot help others and we cannot glorify Jesus.

Israel grieved God the Father, the nine impotent disciples grieved God the Son, and the church today is grieving God the Holy Spirit. "Do not grieve the Holy Spirit of God, by whom you were sealed for the day of redemption" (Eph. 4:30). The Holy Spirit dwells in the body of each true believer and is a person who can be pleased with our obedience and grieved by our disobedience. In his letters to the Ephesians and the Colossians, Paul lists some of the sins that will grieve the Spirit and hinder him from working in us and through us: lying, unrighteous anger, stealing, filthy speech, bitterness, evil speech, and malice. These are inner attitudes that God sees in our hearts and wants to remove before they erupt and cause trouble.

Is Jesus disappointed in us? Are we wearying him with our failures? Are we seeking for "better methods" when God is seeking for better men and women who do not grieve him? "I always do those things that please Him," said Jesus (John 8:29). Let's follow his example.

> Let all bitterness, wrath, anger, clamor, and evil speaking be put away from you, with all malice. And be kind to one another, tenderhearted, forgiving one another, even as God in Christ forgave you.
>
> Ephesians 4:31–32

97

> "*Behold, I send My messenger*, and He will prepare the way before me. And the Lord, whom you seek, will suddenly come to His temple, even the Messenger of the covenant, in whom you delight. Behold, He is coming," says the LORD of hosts.
>
> MALACHI 3:1

Three different messengers are involved in this statement.

The first messenger is Malachi the prophet, because the name *Malachi* means "my messenger." What a privilege it was for him to be God's messenger, to hear his voice and speak and write his words! Malachi's message to the people was not an easy one to deliver, because the people had grown careless and indifferent in their worship of the Lord. To them it was all dull routine, a job to be done. The priests were supposed to serve as the messengers of God (Mal. 2:7), but they had become bored with the temple ministry and were not giving God their best. It didn't upset them that the people brought blind, lame, and sick animals for sacrifices (1:6–8), instead of giving God their finest animals. Some of the people were even bringing animals they had stolen (v. 13)! They had forgotten the words of King David, who would not offer burnt offerings to the Lord of that which had cost him nothing (2 Sam. 24:24). Cheap sacrifices are not sacrifices at all. Have we ever been guilty of this sin?

The second messenger is John the Baptist. "Behold, I send My messenger, and he will prepare the way before Me" (Mal. 3:1). The prophet Isaiah wrote about John: "The voice of one crying in the wilderness, 'Prepare the way of the LORD; make straight in the desert a highway for our God'" (Isa. 40:3; *see* Matt. 3:3). In ancient times, whenever the king planned to visit a city, people went ahead to make sure the roads were cleared of obstacles and made level. John the Baptist was given that ministry. He did not point to himself; he pointed to Jesus, which is what every messenger of the Lord must do. "Behold!" John announced, "The Lamb of God who takes away the sin of the world" (John 1:29). "He must increase, but I must decrease" (3:30). As the King's messengers, we must be faithful to honor the King and not ourselves and to deliver the messages that he has commanded. "For I say to you," Jesus said, "among those born of women there is not a greater prophet than John the Baptist" (Luke 7:28). The Jewish people responded to John's message at the beginning of his ministry, but when he was put in prison, they did nothing to rescue him; he gave his life for his Lord.

The third messenger is our Lord Jesus Christ himself. "And the Lord, whom you seek, will suddenly come to His temple, even the Messenger of the covenant" (Mal. 3:1). Malachi was an official prophet and John the Baptist was born a priest but called to be a prophet, but Jesus is the Prophet, Priest, and King! "And the LORD shall be King over all the earth" (Zech. 14:9). Jesus came to earth the first time to declare the Word of God and accomplish the will of God by dying on the cross for the sins of the world. He will return a second time to judge the world with fire, to purify his people Israel, and to establish his kingdom. Read Zechariah 12–14 and note the repeated phrase "in that day."

The Lord wants his people to be faithful messengers who tell the good news of salvation to others.

> How beautiful upon the mountains
> Are the feet of him who brings good news,
> Who proclaims peace,
> Who brings glad tidings of good things,
> Who proclaims salvation.
>
> Isaiah 52:7

98

Will a man rob God? *Yet you have robbed Me!*
But you say, "In what way have we robbed You?"
In tithes and offerings.

MALACHI 3:8

Christians are *forgiven*, because they have trusted Jesus
Christ and he has forgiven all their sins (Col. 2:13).
Since Christians are forgiven people, they should
also be *forgiving* people (Eph. 4:30–32). And people who are
forgiven and forgiving will also be *for giving*! The grace of
God that has worked in their own hearts should spill over
as they give to others.

God is the generous giver; we must never forget that fact.
"Every good gift and every perfect gift is from above, and
comes down from the Father of lights, with whom there is
no variation or shadow of turning" (James 1:17). "What do
you have that you did not receive?" (1 Cor. 4:7). God "gives
to all life, breath, and all things" (Acts 17:25; *see* 14:17). God
has covenanted with his creation that "seedtime and harvest,
cold and heat, winter and summer, and day and night shall
not cease" (Gen. 8:22). If this were not true, life around the
world would be in chaos, yet we take it all for granted. "If I
were hungry, I would not tell you," God says in Psalm 50:12;
"for the world is Mine, and all its fullness." Before God made
the first man and woman, he prepared a rich and beautiful
home for them in which everything was very good (Gen.
1:31). "He makes His sun rise on the evil and on the good,
and sends rain on the just and on the unjust" (Matt. 5:45).
Over the centuries, the human family has done a great deal
of damage to the creation home God gave us, and we ought
to repent. If we would stop and consider all that the Father
has given us, we would be more generous in giving to others.

God is the generous giver, but man too often is the self-ish robber. People enjoy his gifts, even waste them, and yet forget to give to others or even to give to God. Robbing God is the first human sin recorded in Scripture, when our first parents took the fruit from God's tree and ate it (Gen. 3); and we have been robbing God ever since. The people of Israel were especially guilty of this sin. In the Law of Moses, God commanded the people to bring tithes and offerings to him, promising that he would bless them if they did. "Honor the LORD with your possessions, and with the firstfruits of all your increase; so your barns will be filled with plenty, and your vats will overflow with new wine" (Prov. 3:9–10). In Malachi's time, the Jews robbed God by giving him nothing, by not giving him the very best, and by giving with a grudging spirit. God sees these same sins in his people today. When we rob God, we rob others *and* we rob ourselves! God wants to bless us, but our selfish disobedience grieves him and hinders him from pouring out blessings upon us (Mal. 3:10).

Is there a cure for a selfish heart? Yes! The grace of God. "For you know the grace of our Lord Jesus Christ, that though He was rich, yet for your sakes He became poor, that you through His poverty might become rich" (2 Cor. 8:9). If we are truly experiencing the riches of God's grace, we cannot help but want others to experience it too, and they will if we share with them what God has given to us. By giving to the Lord and to others, we cease to be reservoirs and become channels of blessing. "God is able to make all grace abound toward you, that you, always having all sufficiency in all things, may have an abundance for every good work" (2 Cor. 9:8).

That's quite an arrangement! All grace—abound—all sufficiency—all things—abundance—every good work! We cannot out-give the Lord!

Remember the words of the Lord Jesus, that He said, "It is more blessed to give than to receive."

Acts 20:35

203

99

> Then those who feared the LORD spoke to one another, and *the LORD listened and heard* them; so a book of remembrance was written before Him for those who fear the LORD and who meditate on His name.
>
> MALACHI 3:16

The Jewish people were happy to be away from Babylon and back in their own land, but life there was not easy. The Lord could not bless them as he wanted to because they were not obeying him, so he raised up the prophet Malachi to rebuke them for their sins—at least thirty-six of which are mentioned in the book—and to call them back to sincere devotion to the Lord. The prophet especially rebuked the priests for their carelessness at the altar. The important thing for us today is that we see the Lord in his dealings with his people, for the church today needs to hear and heed Malachi's words.

God regards his people. In spite of the general indifference of the Jewish nation, there was a small group of people who put the Lord first and obeyed him. They feared the Lord (this is mentioned twice) and met together often to encourage one another and meditate on the name of the Lord. "The name of the LORD is a strong tower; the righteous run to it and are safe" (Prov. 18:10). No matter how defiled God's people have become, there has always been a faithful remnant that has honored the Lord, and God has used this remnant to accomplish his will.

God is not impressed with numbers. He trimmed Gideon's army from thirty-two thousand to three hundred and defeated the Midianites (Judg. 7). Jonathan and his armorbearer alone overcame a Philistine garrison, for "nothing restrains the LORD from saving by many or by few" (1 Sam. 14:6). In our statistics-controlled world, we forget Zechariah 4:10, "For who has despised the day of small things?" I often reminded my ministerial students that there are no "small" churches or "big" preachers, only a great and powerful God.

God remembers and records what his people think, say, and do. Jesus is Immanuel, "God with us" (Matt. 1:23), and he promised to be in our midst whenever we assemble in his name (18:20). The metaphor of God keeping records in a book is used frequently in Scripture. "You number my wanderings," wrote David, "put my tears into Your bottle; are they not in Your book?" (Ps. 56:8). He notes where people are born (87:6) and keeps a record of the names of those who are born again (Phil. 4:3; Luke 10:20; Rev. 21:27). Whether God's people gather in Christ's name in a private home, a simple hall, or a great cathedral, we must remember that the Lord is there with us and "Nothing in all creation is hidden from God's sight. Everything is uncovered and laid bare before the eyes of him to whom we must give account" (Heb. 4:13 TNIV). At the judgment seat of Christ, our works will be reviewed and we will be rewarded accordingly (Rom. 14:10–12). How important it is that we fear the Lord as we worship, hear the Scriptures read and expounded, and fellowship with one another.

God rewards the faithful. "'They shall be mine,' says the Lord of hosts, 'on the day that I make them My jewels'" (Mal. 3:17). The word *jewels* may also be translated "treasures." The people of Israel were indeed a treasure of the Lord, even though they did not always appreciate it or act like it (Exod. 19:5; Deut. 7:6; 14:2). The church is also a special treasure of the Lord, purchased by the precious blood of Jesus Christ (1 Pet. 1:19). We may be part of a minority, but we are valuable to our Father in heaven. He loves us, sees us, hears us, looks into our hearts, and will one day reward us to the glory of his Son. What encouragement it is to know that he is watching and listening, and he knows our hearts.

The Lord . . . will both bring to light the hidden things of darkness and reveal the counsels of the hearts. Then each one's praise will come from God.

1 Corinthians 4:5

100

> "*Behold, the day is coming*, burning like an oven, and all the proud, yes, all who do wickedly will be stubble. And the day which is coming shall burn them up," says the LORD of hosts. . . . "But to you who fear My name the Sun of Righteousness shall arise with healing in His wings."
>
> MALACHI 4:1–2

What day is coming? The day of the Lord, the day when he judges the inhabitants of the earth. The phrase "in that day" is found sixteen times in Zechariah 12–14 as the prophet describes what will happen when "there will be no more delay" (Rev. 10:6 TNIV). Note the contrasts in our text.

The unbelieving wicked and the God-fearing righteous. In New Testament language, "the lost" and "the saved," those who have rejected Christ and those who have received him. Jesus makes it clear that there are only two "ways" of life: the narrow way of faith in Christ and the broad, popular way of the world that rejects Christ (Matt. 7:13–14). "For the LORD knows the way of the righteous, but the way of the ungodly shall perish" (Ps. 1:6). Who are the righteous? All who have repented of their sins and trusted Christ alone for salvation. Who are the ungodly? All who have never trusted Christ but rely on their good works and religious activities to save them. We do not become children of God by good works but by trusting in the finished work of Jesus on the cross. "But God demonstrates His own love toward us, in that while we were still sinners, Christ died for us" (Rom. 5:8).

The burning oven and the healing sun (Mal. 4:2). "I am the light of the world," Jesus said. "He who follows Me shall not walk in darkness, but have the light of life" (John 8:12). During those awful days of tribulation, the Lord will pour out his wrath on a sinful world, and this will include scorching heat from the sun. "The men were scorched with great heat, and they blasphemed the name of God, who has power over these plagues; and they did not repent and give Him glory" (Rev. 16:9). The sun is a picture of Jesus Christ (Isa. 9:1–2; Matt. 4:16). He heals his own people but judges those who reject him. "You shall make them as a fiery oven in the time of Your anger; the LORD shall swallow them up in His wrath" (Ps. 21:9). God is not only love but is also light (1 John 1:5; 4:8); he loves the sinner but must judge the sins. If we trust Jesus, in his holy love he will forgive us and heal us of our sins. Jesus is "the Dayspring from on high" who has visited us and died for us on the cross (Luke 1:78). What will it be for you: burning or healing?

The burned stubble and the skipping calf (Mal. 4:3). The prophet pictures the unbeliever as stubble or chaff that is burned up and trodden down, while the believer is like a lively calf that is let out of the pen and skips joyfully across the ground, trampling on the stubble! Today, unbelieving sinners think they are the winners and that Christians are fools, but the day is coming when the "great" will be like burned stubble and the meek will inherit the earth. Calves are kept in pens to be fattened up for slaughter, but not the people of the Lord! They are set free to frisk under "the Sun of Righteousness . . . with healing in His wings" (v. 2).

Malachi ends his book with an ominous statement from the Lord: "lest I come and strike the earth with a curse" (v. 6). But believers aren't frightened by this statement because, near the close of the New Testament, the Lord says "there shall be no more curse" (Rev. 22:3).

"Behold, the day is coming," and we had better be prepared.

> And the LORD shall be King over all the earth.
> In that day it shall be—
> "The LORD is one,"
> And His name one.
>
> Zechariah 14:9

Warren W. Wiersbe has served as a pastor, radio Bible teacher, and seminary instructor and is the author of more than 150 books, including the popular BE series of Bible expositions. He pastored the Moody Church in Chicago and also ministered with Back to the Bible Broadcast for ten years, five of them as Bible teacher and general director. His conference ministry has taken him to many countries. He and his wife, Betty, make their home in Lincoln, Nebraska, where he continues his writing ministry.